IRISH-AMERICAN FUNNY QUOTES

• • • • •

Merrit Malloy

Sterling Publishing Co., Inc.
New York

Library of Congress Cataloging-in-Publication Data

Irish-American funny quotes / [compiled] by Merrit Malloy.
     p.   cm.
    Includes index.
    ISBN 0-8069-0753-3
    1. Quotations, English–Irish authors. 2. Irish Americans—
Quotations. 3. Irish-American wit and humor. I. Malloy, Merrit.
PN6084.I6I6   1994
082'.0899162073—dc29   94–26206
                                          CIP

10 9 8 7 6 5 4 3 2 1

Published by Sterling Publishing Company, Inc.
387 Park Avenue South, New York, N.Y. 10016
© 1994 by Merrit Malloy
Distributed in Canada by Sterling Publishing
℅ Canadian Manda Group, One Atlantic Avenue, Suite 105
Toronto, Ontario, Canada M6K 3E7
Distributed in Great Britain and Europe by Cassell PLC
Villiers House, 41/47 Strand, London WC2N 5JE, England
Distributed in Australia by Capricorn Link (Australia) Pty Ltd.
P.O. Box 6651, Baulkham Hills, Business Centre, NSW 2153, Australia
Manufactured in the United States of America
All rights reserved

Sterling ISBN 0-8069-0753-3

CONTENTS

PROLOGUE

A remarkable number of Americans claim to be Irish, partly Irish, a little bit Irish, etc. Never mind that their names end in "sky" or "ione," they're proud of their Irishness, in spite of its other than Irish origin. (It's said that the Norwegian Irish are twice unique, since many of them are Lutheran too; somebody once said this was why the Norwegian Irish can play heartbreaking music on the cello, but sadly they can't hear it themselves.)

Back to the point—Irishness and the many claims to being Irish—especially when it's just good business sense and always around St. Patty's Day when (truly) everybody actually is Irish (no kidding—a priest told me).

Someone I know said he once saw Charles Revson (that's right, the same man who installed a fountain in New York's Lincoln Center with the gold-embossed words "Placed here in honor of Charles Revson by the Charles Revson Foundation") interrupt a meeting of the Irish Development Association to complain that not enough was being done to encourage investment in his Irish homeland. (His Irish what?)

And, of course, you may remember when President Nixon, struggling for votes, went himself (the dear boy) to the auld sod of motherland herself to proclaim his "oh, so Kennedy-like" roots. He found them, as he made "perfectly clear" on the six o'clock news during a campaign.

So, you see my problem here in compiling a book of authentic Irish-Americans. Indeed, with all the many months of extensive research, I still can't be absolutely certain that every single name included in this book is Irish. I'm mostly certain that they are, but over time I've found many, many celebrities who have changed their names from Goldberg to O'Riley, and the other way around.

I have run across some "Sure sounds like she is, but she isn't." And there has yet to be a politician on the stump who was not at least a little bit Irish. Black, yellow, or beige, it makes no difference. They all have a touch of the old blarney (which is just Irish for charisma), they all love the lilt of the language, and they remember the poignant words—"O Danny Boy, O Danny Boy, I love you so. ..."

So, this is just to say that, here and there, I may have been fooled. For all my so-called sophistication and savvy, I too have the curse and the blessing of being Irish—Irish on all sides, inside out, and all around. It's the best thing and the worst thing that can ever happen.

Erin go bragh!
Merrit Malloy

CALIFORNIA/HOLLYWOOD/L.A.

Nothing is wrong with Southern California that a rise in the ocean level wouldn't cure. —*Ross McDonald*

What with the Los Angeles earthquake, massive forest fires, beach erosion, freeway shootings, and ozone-layer depletion that's giving Malibu volleyball players whole-body melanoma, it looks like God has finally gotten serious about destroying California. Sources close to the Lord say the so-called "yuppie shows" of the new T.V. season were the last straw.

—*P. J. O'Rourke*

If you stay in Beverly Hills too long you become a Mercedes.

—*Robert Redford*

Finish your vegetables! There are children in Beverly Hills with eating disorders. —*John Callahan*

If my books had been any worse I would not have been invited to Hollywood, and if they had been any better I would not have come. —*Raymond Chandler*

The eleventh commandment of a motion picture negotiation: Thou shalt not take less than thy last deal. —*John Gregory Dunne*

I've got friends in this town that I haven't even used yet.

—*Bobby Logan (facetiously, it's presumed)*

Hollywood is like Picasso's bathroom. —*Candice Bergen*

These are an ignorant lot of bastards. —*John Ford (on Hollywood)*

The best things in movies happen by accident. —*John Ford*

You can take all the sincerity in Hollywood, place it in the navel of a fruit fly, and still have room enough for three car-away seeds and a producer's heart. —*Fred Allen*

California is all right for Californians. The people who rave about it are the people who came from someplace worse.

—*Preston Sturges*

California is a great place to live if you're an orange.

—*Fred Allen*

Historians have now definitely established that Juan Cabrillo, discoverer of California, was not looking for Kansas, thus setting a precedent that continues to this day.   —*Wayne Shannon*

FASHION

Esquire is always on the cutting edge of twerpiness. It's a magazine read by men who actually worry about whether their socks are out of style.   —*P. J. O'Rourke*

By next winter, the only practical accessory for a fur coat will be earplugs.   —*Dan Matthews*

Them as has 'em wears 'em.

—*"Diamond" Jim Brady (on diamonds, of course)*

Her hat is a creation that will never go out of style. It will look just as ridiculous year after year.   —*Fred Allen*

Women's clothes: never wear anything that panics the cat.

—*P. J. O'Rourke*

COMPLAINTS

My family worked for everything we had. We even had a deed from the King of England for property in South Carolina. Now these jerks come along and try to give it to the Communists.

—*Martha Mitchell*

I'm tired of everlastingly being unnatural and never doing anything I want to do. I'm tired of acting like I don't eat more than a bird and walking when I want to run and saying I feel faint after a waltz when I could dance for two days and never get tired. I'm tired of saying "How wonderful you are!" to fool men who haven't got one-half the sense I've got, and I'm tired of pretending I don't know anything, so men can tell me things and feel important while they're doing it. ...

—*Margaret Mitchell (Scarlett O'Hara, in "Gone with the Wind")*

Everything takes longer than it takes.   —*Murphy's Law*

THE IRISH ON OTHERS

The Secret Service is under orders that if Bush is shot, to shoot Quayle. —*John Kerry (Massachusetts senator)*

I would not put Jimmy Carter in charge of snake control in Ireland. —*Eugene McCarthy*

His [President Warren G. Harding's] speeches left the impression of an army of pompous phrases moving over the landscape in search of an idea; sometimes these meandering words would actually capture a straggling thought and bear it triumphantly, a prisoner in their midst, until it died of servitude and overwork. —*William G. McAdoo*

Racial characteristics [of the English]: cold blooded queers with nasty complexions and terrible teeth who once conquered half the world but still haven't figured out central heating. They warm their beers and chill their baths and boil all their food, including bread. —*P. J. O'Rourke*

She knows, better than most women, that we must never let the men have the last word. They always get it wrong. —*Jane O'Reilly (about Martha Gellhorn)*

[Arnold] Rothstein is a man who dwells in doorways. A mouse standing in a doorway, waiting for his cheese. —*William Fallon (on the legendary engineer of the infamous Chicago "Black Socks" scandal)*

She [Eleanor Roosevelt] got even in a way that was almost cruel. She forgave them. —*Ralph McGill*

Eisenhower is the only living Unknown Soldier. —*Robert S. Kerr (Oklahoma senator)*

[He's a] Boy Scout with a hormonal imbalance. —*Kevin Phillips (of George Bush)*

I was a little disappointed in that movie "The Last Emperor." I thought it was going to be about Don Regan. —*Ronald Reagan*

Gene Mauch's stare can put you on the disabled list. —*Tim McCarver*

He doesn't seem to stand for anything.

> —*Ronald Reagan (of George Bush, as quoted in "The Washington Post," March 1982; he later denied making this remark)*

I never knew that ✳✳✳✳ [John Wayne] could act.

> —*John Ford (after seeing "Red River"; Ford had already used Wayne in many of his classic films, including "Stagecoach")*

You know, your nose looks just like Danny Thomas's.

> —*Ronald Reagan (to the Lebanese foreign minister)*

THE IRISH ON THE IRISH

The people from Mayo are noted for their shrewdness and smartness. We're a smart, shrewd, poor race. Proud as hell. You don't say "County Mayo," but "County Mayo, God help us."
> —*John Ford*

I can't even recall one Irish name among the many thousands called before the House Committee on Un-American Activities. If there was, he probably changed his name.
> —*Thomas Murphy*

The Irish are the damnedest race. They put so much emphasis on so many wrong things.
> —*Margaret Mitchell (from "Gone with the Wind")*

ON BEING IRISH

I'm Irish. Country music is Irish music. Appalachian music was brought over by the Scotch and the Irish.   —*Eddie Rabbit*

To be Irish is to be twice-blessed: first as a life, then as a "liver" of life.   —*Bridget O'Donnell*

Being Irish is like belonging to a secret club. It's impossible to say it, but it's true. Being Irish is being just a taste more possible in impossible situations.   —*Alisha (Riley) Everett*

The wonder is not that the Irish hate the English, but that they really don't hate them.   —*Andrew Greeley*

To the Irish, life is a tragedy and a comedy; to Lutherans, it is just a tragedy.   —*Bridget O'Donnell*

I come from an Irish family in Brooklyn, a few stockbrokers, a smattering of intellectuals …and forty percent of the New York police force. My uncle the cop used to read me bedtime stories: "Humpty Dumpty sat on the wall, Humpty Dumpty fell— or was pushed—from the wall. The perpetrator has not been apprehended. Three male Hispanics were seen leaving the area."   —*Colin Quinn*

For many of us Americans, there is a gap between our past and our present, between our childhood and our productive manhood. We are the sons and daughters, the grandsons and granddaughters, of the disinherited earth. Our forebears partook little of the great culture of mankind. Their lives and destinies were hard; their contributions to our civilization were made with their backs. We have come from their poverty. We have a personal past different from the past suggested in the great and inspiring world of culture and ideas. Our beginnings were naive, and we must still understand the difference between our present and our past.   —*James T. Farrell*

Everybody's Irish on St. Patty's Day.   —*Helen O'Donnell Malloy*

Memories

Returning to Washington today really brought back memories. As our plane headed to the airport, I looked down on the White House and it was just like the good old days—the South Lawn, the Rose Garden, David Gergen.

—*Ronald Reagan (in 1994)*

Nostalgia is longing for something you couldn't stand anymore.   —*Fibber McGee (Jim Jordan)*

When you have committed an action that you cannot bear to think about, that causes you to writhe in retrospect, do not seek to evade the memory: make yourself relive it, confront it repeatedly over and over, till finally, you will discover, through sheer repetition it loses its power to pain you. It works, I guarantee you, this surefire guilt-eradicator, like a homeopathic medicine—like in small doses applied to like. It works, but I am not sure that is a good thing.   —*Mary McCarthy*

What beastly incidents our memories insist on cherishing—the ugly and disgusting—the beautiful things we have to keep diaries to remember.   —*Eugene O'Neill*

I can remember her just as if it was yesterday. ... Our first meeting. It was in the park. She coyly dropped her handkerchief. And as I picked it up, she was embarrassed. Her nose was still in it.   —*Jackie Gleason (on first love)*

MISSTATEMENTS/BLUNDERS

This is a great day for France!
                            —*Richard Nixon (at de Gaulle's funeral)*

Now we are trying to get unemployment to go up, and I think we are going to succeed.   —*Ronald Reagan*

Lead us in a few words of silent prayer.   —*Bill Peterson*

As the Reagan presidency ends, it is time for the Bush pregnancy to begin.   —*Tommy Thompson (Wisconsin governor)*

Man has been given his freedom to greater extent than ever and that's quite wrong.   —*Martha Mitchell*

This is the worst disaster in California since I was elected.
               —*Pat Brown (California governor, regarding a flood)*

Gerald Ford was a Communist.
                            —*Ronald Reagan (in a speech; he later indicated that he meant to say congressman)*

Do you come here often?
  —*Edward M. (Ted) Kennedy (to a patron of a Brooklyn soup kitchen)*

ABOUT THE IRISH

What a time to have an Irish president!
                    —*Pierre Salinger (on the Cuban missile crisis)*

Ronald Reagan doesn't dye his hair—he's just prematurely orange.   —*Gerald Ford*

Ask him the time, and he'll tell you how the watch was made.
                    —*Jane Wyman, former wife of Ronald Reagan*

A triumph of the embalmer's art.

—*Gore Vidal (of Ronald Reagan)*

Other people have a nationality. The Irish and the Jews have a psychosis.   —*Brendan Behan*

Gladstone spent his declining years trying to guess the answer to the Irish question; unfortunately, whenever he was getting warm, the Irish secretly changed the question.

—*W. C. Sellers (British humorist)*

The Irish don't know what they want and are prepared to fight to the death to get it.   —*Sidney Littlewood*

I never met anyone in Ireland who understood the Irish question, except one Englishman who had only been there a week.

—*Keith Fraser (British politician)*

The problem with Ireland (the Irish) is that it's a country full of geniuses, but with absolutely no talent.

—*Hugh Leonard (Irish dramatist)*

The English should give Ireland home rule—and reserve the motion picture rights.   —*Will Rogers*

All races have produced notable economists, with the exception of the Irish, who doubtless can protest their devotion to higher arts.   —*John Kenneth Galbraith*

The English and the Americans dislike only some Irish: the same Irish that the Irish themselves detest, Irish writers—the ones that think.   —*Brendan Behan*

Voodoo economics.

—*George Bush (referring to Ronald Reagan's eco-nomic policies during the 1980 presidential election)*

If you take a black left hand and a white right hand and put them together, you've got rock 'n' roll. And that's Jerry Lee.

—*Jim McBride (of Jerry Lee Lewis)*

If he had ever told the truth and faced his demons, he would have been one of the greatest creatures on this planet.

—*Ali MacGraw (of Steve McQueen)*

Like Odysseus, he looked wiser when seated.

> —*John Maynard Keynes (of Woodrow Wilson)*

The enviable attractive nephew who sings an Irish ballad for the company and then disappears before the table-clearing and dishwashing begins.   —*Lyndon Johnson (of J.F.K.)*

Fitzgerald was an alcoholic, a spendthrift, and a superstar playboy possessed of a beauty and a glamour that only a Byron could support without artistic ruination.

> —*Anthony Burgess (of F. Scott Fitzgerald)*

Nixon is the kind of politician who would cut down a redwood tree and then mount the stump to make a speech for conservation.   —*Adlai Stevenson*

President Nixon's motto was, if two wrongs don't make a right, try three.   —*Norman Cousins*

Mary Robinson is not only Ireland's first woman president, she is virtually the only president anyone can remember.   —*Vogue*

It's an Irish tradition to want to take people down a peg.

> —*Kenneth Branagh*

ART

Making your unknown known is the important thing—and keeping the unknown always beyond you.   —*Georgia O'Keeffe*

When she was here, the place was magical. Now it's just three funny buildings.   —*Diana MacKeon (of Louise Nevelson)*

In cats, art becomes visible.   —*M. Malloy*

The artist in his teens who is happy is a charlatan. Life comes bursting in all around us too suddenly, too crudely, too cruelly, for happiness.   —*William McFee*

For the mystic, what is how. For the craftsman, how is what. For the artist, what and how are one.   —*William McElcheran*

Art is not reality—by definition, it is not reality.   —*Bob McKee*

BEAUTY

My gift is that I'm not beautiful. My career was never about looks. It's about health and being in good shape.

—*Shirley MacLaine*

I'm tired of all this nonsense about beauty being only skin-deep. That's deep enough. What do you want, an adorable pancreas?

—*Jean Kerr*

If love is blind, why are so many men attracted to a beautiful woman?

—*E. C. McKenzie*

It is easy to be beautiful; it is difficult to appear so. —*Frank O'Hara*

People have been so busy relating to how I look, it's a miracle I didn't become a self-conscious blob of protoplasm.

—*Robert Redford*

THE UNEXAMINED LIFE

I don't feel guilty that five or ten generations ago these people were slaves. Now, I'm not condoning slavery. It's just a fact of life.

—*John Wayne*

I can't get over saying "colored." I said it all my life. All the Negroes seem to resent it, and I don't know why.

—*Martha Mitchell*

It's not listed in the Bible, but my spiritual gift, my specific calling from God, is to be a television talk-show host.

—*James Bakker (former TV evangelist)*

TV/TECHNOLOGY

The cable TV sex channels don't expand our horizons, don't make us better people, don't come in clearly enough.

—*Bill Maher*

When I feel like getting away from it all, I just turn the TV on to a Spanish soap opera and imagine I'm on vacation in a hotel in Mexico.

—*Brian McKim*

Cats think Beavis and Butt-head are a mistake.

—*Nan "Swifty" Porter*

The stories we do are real. We do not do aliens eating babies.
—*Maureen O'Boyle (host of "A Current Affair")*

Anyone who likes golf on television would enjoy watching the grass grow on the greens. —*Andy Rooney*

You know, I've always wondered about the taping equipment. But I'm damn glad we have it. —*Richard Nixon*

STATISTICS

Facts are stupid things. —*Ronald Reagan (misquoting John Adams: "Facts are stubborn things. ... ")*

Facts are neutral. —*Bob McKee*

Statistics are used like a drunk uses a lamppost—for support, not illumination. —*Vin Scully*

One fifth of the people are against everything all the time.
—*Robert F. Kennedy*

ADVICE

Never sleep with anyone who has more problems than you do.
—*Bob McKee*

Go to bed. What you're staying up for isn't worth it.
—*Andy Rooney*

Follow the rules of holes: If you are in one, stop digging.
—*Dennis Healy*

I have only one training rule: Don't get caught.
—*Frank McGuire*

If you wish to live wisely, ignore sayings—including this one.
—*Heywood (Hale) Broun*

It's much wiser to love thy neighbor than his wife.
—*E. C. McKenzie*

Acquire an incurable ailment in your youth.
—*James Cardinal Gibbons (advice on a long life)*

Remember you can publish and perish. —*Bob McKee*

Never try to smash a lawyer in the face. You might hurt yourself. —*Pete Ferguson*

Never eat in a restaurant where you see a cockroach bench-pressing a burrito. —*Pat McCormick*

[On coping with the pressure of new stardom] Start with one thing: that they need you. Without you they have an empty screen. So, when you get on there, just do what you think is right and stay with it. From that point on, you're on your own. … If you listen to all the clowns around you're just dead. Go do what you have to do. —*James Cagney (advice to John Travolta)*

It's totally okay to be a normie. —*Drew Barrymore*

In the matter of ideas, he who meditates is lost. —*William McFee*

Beware of immediate reactions.
—*Richard J. Riordan (Los Angeles mayor)*

If it's not working, plug it in. —*An Irish Sears repairman*

Life is easier than you'd think; all that is necessary is to accept the impossible, do without the indispensable, and bear the intolerable. —*Kathleen Norris*

Leave well—even "pretty well"—alone: that is what I learn as I get old. —*Edward Fitzgerald*

MELANCHOLY

What's the use of being Irish if the world doesn't break your heart? —*John F. Kennedy*

For me, singing sad songs often has a way of healing a situation. It gets the hurt out in the open—into the light, out of the darkness. —*Reba McEntire*

In a real dark night of the soul it is always three o'clock in the morning, day after day. —*F. Scott Fitzgerald*

Christmas has given me nothing but a flair for inventive suicides since I passed the sad years of that holiday at the age of nine. —*Jim Carroll*

MUSIC/MUSICIANS

I was involved in the "great folk music scare" back in the sixties. When it *almost* caught on. It was close for a time, but fortunately ...
                                                              —*Martin Mull*

I have often thought that if there had been a good rap group around in those days, I would have chosen a career in music instead of politics.

—*Richard Nixon (1990, in a tape-recorded tour of the Nixon Library)*

The [Rolling] Stones aren't playing rock 'n' roll any more. They are playing for Budweiser.   —*Singer Mike O'Connell*

By the time Beethoven died, he was so deaf, he thought he was an artist.   —*Pat McCormick*

I have, on occasion, sacrificed myself and my own emotional makeup, singing "I'm selfish and I'm sad," for instance. These are not attractive things in the context of rock 'n' roll—which is "Honey, I'm a lover and I'm bad!"   —*Joni Mitchell*

Music helps set a romantic mood. Some men believe the only good music is live music. Imagine her surprise when you say, "I don't need a stereo—I have an accordion!" Then imagine the sound of a door slamming.   —*Martin Mull*

I like acting, but in no way am I putting down my guitar. That's reality. The rest is Hollywood.   —*David Crosby*

We, Barry Melton and myself, finally signed a piece of paper which he interprets as saying that he is the Fish. So when we play together in a week or so, it'll be "Country Joe" McDonald and Barry "the Fish" Melton. It's evolved to that. He's become a lawyer, so we don't argue with him anymore.

—*Country Joe McDonald*

We did consider the name "Beetles," but Jerry [Allison] said, "Aw, that's just a bug you'd want to step on," so we immediately dropped that.   —*Niki Sullivan (on the naming of Buddy Holly's backup band the Crickets.)*

NEW YORK

I've been a New Yorker for ten years, and the only people who are nice to us turn out to be Moonies.   —*P. J. O'Rourke*

I could never play in New York. The first time I ever came into a game there, I got in the bullpen car and they told me to lock the door.   —*Mike Flanagan*

When you leave New York, you're camping out. —*Jackie Gleason*

New York is like living inside Steven King's brain during an aneurysm. It's the Land of the Genetic Close Calls. There are a lot of people there who missed being another species by one chromosome. Look—that guy could've been a badger. There's Crab Man. ...And it's like a financial skeet shoot. Someone hollers "Pull!" and your wallet flies out.   —*Kevin Rooney*

I come from New York, where if you fall down someone will pick up your wallet.   —*Al McGuire*

I didn't bet him anything. New York doesn't have anything I want.
   —*Ann Richards, Texas governor, regarding Mario Cuomo's giving*
       her a bouquet of yellow roses after the Dallas Cowboys Super Bowl

A woman on the Fifth Avenue bus was being a nuisance. Every five minutes she'd pester the driver, "Are we on Riverside Drive yet?" She kept asking, getting on his nerves, but he kept his temper. When he didn't respond after she asked yet again, she cried, "How will I know when we come to Riverside Drive?" He said, "By the big smile on my face, lady, by the big smile on my face."   —*Frank Sullivan*

I wasn't happy about the phoniness that I was feeling in L.A., the emphasis on money, the emphasis on what kind of car you drive, the cultural lack. I always knew that I wanted to try to live here [Manhattan], because I felt that I could do anything. I could go to acting classes, I could go to museums, I could take singing classes, the kids could talk to the doormen, talk to taxi drivers, talk to everyone, all of us getting stimulated.
   —*Tatum O'Neal*

19

New Yorkers love it when you spill your guts out there. You spill your guts at Wimbledon, they make you stop and clean it up.   —*Jimmy Connors*

FEMINISTS

In the past, a man was expected to give his seat to a woman. Today, it would be much more courteous for that man to give her his job.   —*P. J. O'Rourke*

For me, self-knowledge could only begin because there is a feminist movement.   —*Susan Griffin*

We have not owned our freedom long enough to know exactly how it should be used.   —*Phyllis McGinley*

MOTIVATION

The best way to get husbands to do anything is to suggest that perhaps they're too old to do it.   —*Shirley MacLaine*

I hate losing more than I love winning.   —*Jimmy Connors*

With enough coffee, you can do anything.   —*Bob McKee*

My purpose is to entertain myself first and other people secondly.   —*John D. MacDonald*

OLD IRISH

[The Irish American situation] is one of shame and poverty. … "My master is great tyrant," said a Negro lately, "he treats me as badly as if I was a common Irishman."
                                    —*Patrick Murphy (1851)*

There are Russian Socialists and Jewish Socialists and German Socialists! But, thank God! There are no Irish Socialists.
    —*George B. McClellan (New York mayor; from a 1907 speech that led directly to the formation of the Irish Socialist Federation.)*

One thing I think is certain, that if emigrants knew beforehand what they have to suffer for about the first six months after leaving home in every respect, they would never come here. However, an enterprising man desirous of advancing himself in the world will despise everything for coming to this free country, where a man is allowed to thrive and flourish without having a penny taken out of his pocket by government; no visits from tax gatherers, constables, or soldiers, every one at liberty to act and speak as he likes, provided he does not hurt another, to slander and damn government, abuse public men in their office to their faces, wear your hat in court and smoke a cigar while speaking to the judge as familiarly as if he was a common mechanic, hundreds go unpunished for crimes for which they would be surely hung in Ireland; in fact, they are so tender of life in this country that a person should have a very great interest to get himself hanged for anything.

—*John Doyle (in a letter from a recent immigrant to his wife, c. 1818)*

My principles and my sufferings were my first passport and introduction here, and they procured me that effective regard of the leading characters of this state and in the Union at large. In proportion as I cherish these principles I am respected, and every day's reflection and observation makes them dearer to me. Ought I go where they are treasonable and sufficient ground for perpetual proscription? … As to my children, I hope they will love liberty too much ever to fix a voluntary residence in an enslaved country.

—*Thomas Addis Emmett (Irish immigrant who rose to become attorney general of New York state)*

CYNICISM

I don't know what it is, but I can't look at Hulk Hogan and believe that he's the end result of millions and millions of years of evolution. —*Jim Murray*

There are a number of mechanical devices which increase sexual arousal, particularly in women. Chief among these is the Mercedes-Benz 380SL convertible. —*P. J. O'Rourke*

You have to give Pete credit for what he's accomplished. He never went to college, and the only book he ever read was "The Pete Rose Story." —*Karolyn Rose (the former wife of Pete Rose)*

Don't jump on a man unless he's down. —*Finley Peter Dunne*

Revise and revise and revise—the best thought will come after the printer has snatched away the copy.   —*Michael Monahan*

I'd rather find out my wife was cheating on me than to keep losing like this. At least I could tell my wife to cut it out.
—*Tom McVie*

In the final analysis, it's true that fame is unimportant. No matter how great a man is, the size of his funeral usually depends on the weather.   —*Rosemary Clooney*

I have just returned from Boston. It is the only thing to do if you find yourself there.   —*Fred Allen*

Football is a game designed to keep coal miners off the streets.
—*Jimmy Breslin*

SOLITUDE

Certain springs are tapped only when we are alone. ... Women need solitude in order to find again the true essence of themselves; that firm strand which will be the indispensable center of a whole web of human relationships.
—*Anne Morrow Lindbergh*

Yet who could deny that privacy is a jewel? It has always been the mark of privilege, the distinguishing feature of a truly urbane culture.   —*Phyllis McGinley*

Once you have lived with another, it is a great torture to have to live alone.   —*Carson McCullers*

Only one hour in the normal day is more pleasurable than the hour spent in bed with a book before going to sleep and that is the hour spent in bed with a book after being called in the morning.   —*Rose Macaulay*

CARS

Lemons are not always yellow.   —*Molly (Malloy) Wiest*

Some people say a front-engine car handles best. Some people say a rear-engine car handles best. I say a rented car handles best.   —*P. J. O'Rourke*

Hood ornaments. They were just lovely and they gave a sense of respect. And they took 'em away because if you can save one human life—that's always the argument—it's worth it, if you can save one human life. Actually, I'd be willing to trade maybe a dozen human lives for a nice hood ornament. I imagine those things really did tend to stick in bicyclists.

—Michael O'Donoghue

The car has become a secular sanctuary for the individual, his shrine to the self, his mobile Walden Pond. *—Edward McDonagh*

A car is useless in New York, essential everywhere else. The same with good manners. *—Mignon McLaughlin*

Some people have a lot of vanity. They say, "I only wear glasses when I drive." If you only need glasses when you drive, then drive around with a prescription windshield! *—Brian Regan*

An American always makes sure his car is working, whether he is or not. *—E. C. McKenzie*

BIRTH/PREGNANCY

I'm pregnant. No need to applaud; I was asleep at the time.
—Jeannie McBride

In the sheltered simplicity of the first days after a baby is born, one sees again the magical closed circle. The miraculous sense of two people existing only for each other.

—Anne Morrow Lindbergh

The thing about having a baby is that thereafter you have it.
—Jean Kerr

Ladies and gentlemen, I would like to introduce my sister, who is representing my wife, who is otherwise committed.

—John F. Kennedy (Jacqueline Kennedy was absent from the 1960 campaign appearance in Oregon due to her pregnancy)

COMMUNICATION

If people can't communicate, then the least they can do is shut up. *—Tom Lehrer*

Many are called, but few are called back.
—*Sister Mary Tricky (from a cartoon by Mary Malloy)*

I think the reason I still love him is that I have no communication with him.
—*Carol Matthau*

No one really listens to anyone else, and if you try it for a while you'll see why.
—*Mignon McLaughlin*

To those who say it is time to reform this organization and that it's time the officers stopped selling out its members, I say, "Go to hell."
—*Frank Fitzsimmons (Teamsters president)*

Good communication is as stimulating as black coffee, and just as hard to sleep after.
—*Anne Morrow Lindbergh*

Anything that can be misunderstood has been misunderstood.
—*Murphy's Law*

HORSE SENSE

You just walk up there and hit it.
—*Hugh Duffy*

Stories are metaphors for life.
—*Bob McKee*

Don't cut off your nose yourself.
—*Casey Stengel*

Don't hurry. Don't worry. You're only here for a short visit. So don't forget to stop and smell the roses.
—*Walter Hagan (golfer)*

Everything takes longer than it should, with the possible exception of sex.
—*Jim McGinn (McGinn's Law #1)*

I've got a tooth that's driving me to extraction.
—*Charlie McCarthy*

Speeches are like babies—easy to conceive but hard to deliver.
—*Pat O'Malley*

For God's sake, don't do it unless you have to. ... It's not easy. It shouldn't be easy, but it shouldn't be impossible, and it's damn near impossible.
—*Frank Conroy (on life and acting)*

Old-timers' games, weekends, and airplane landings are alike. If you can walk away from them, they're successful.
—*Casey Stengel*

Beware of cats that bark. —*Bridget O'Donnell*

Tell the truth. It's cheaper than an attorney and a lot more effective. —*Merrit Malloy*

We must not be innocents abroad in a world that is not innocent. —*Ronald Reagan*

We have only one bathroom, so you'll have to take pot luck.
—*Frank Sullivan*

When Eve asked Adam, "Do you love me?" Adam answered, "Who else?" —*Larry Wilde*

SURVIVAL

As a heterosexual ballet dancer, you develop a thick skin.
—*Ronald (Ron) Reagan Jr.*

Every woman who writes is a survivor. —*Tillie Olson*

Does it bother me? Oh, yes. Does it hurt sometimes? Absolutely. But I learned a long time ago not to expect to be treated fairly. I expect to survive and I will.
—*Kathleen Sullivan (journalist; reacting to comments on her becoming the spokesperson for Weight Watchers)*

When you get to the end of your rope, tie a knot in it so's you can hang on. —*James Mitchell*

We cannot count on the instinct for survival to protect us against war. —*Ronald Reagan*

I guarantee to survive and I guarantee that my bones dissolving into chalky dust will fight them from the grave.
—*James T. Farrell*

DOGS

Dogs are "Co-dependent," cats are "In-dependent," and we humans are hovering somewhere in between. —*Charlie Quackenbush*

It was so hot out today, I saw a Dalmatian with his spots on the ground. —*Pat McCormick*

It takes a heap of liver to make a dog a home.

—*Fibber McGee (Jim Jordan)*

I named my all my dogs with my heart, but I always named the cats for themselves. —*Murphy Malloy Kall*

CATS

Garfield's Law: Cats instinctively know the precise moment their owners will awaken ... then they awaken them ten minutes sooner. —*Jim Davis*

Cats are sculpture set to music. —*M. Malloy*

If there is one spot of sun spilling onto the floor, a cat will find it and soak it up. —*Joan Asper McIntosh*

Cats understand every word we don't say. —*Merrit Malloy*

Cats—one of the few things in life that, if they didn't exist, not even Robin Williams could make them up.

—*Mitchell (James) Miller*

I saw a commercial the other day for cat food. It said, "All natural food for your cat." All-natural food. But cat food is made out of horse meat. That's how it works in nature—the cat is right above the horse on the food chain. ... Matter of fact, every time my kitty feels a little cooped up in his environment, I take him down to the racetrack, let him stalk some prey.

—*Norm McDonald*

If cats could talk, they wouldn't . —*Nan "Swifty" Porter*

Cats are simply articles of commerce. We can purchase them. This, I suspect, is what has caused them, as a species, to regard humans with disdain. It must certainly appear to them as though we are the animals. —*Bridget O'Donnell*

Cats are like the phone company: They'll cut you off if you won't play by their rules. —*Garrison "Blue" Reed*

I purr, therefore I am.—*Merrit Malloy (from CAT Philosophy Book)*

Cats have nine lives, fleas have ten. —*Brian Walsh*

Crazy cats have three eyes? —*Kit (Sheehan)Yuen*

If cats ran the world, it would make sense but it wouldn't have to. —*Mac O'Brian Wiest*

I don't love cats because they're beautiful, I love them because they are authentic and true to themselves. —*Alisha Everett*

We make plans and cats laugh. —*Jeremy Ben Lindsey*

You can't train cats. Even though they are often quite talented, they're much too smart to do tricks. —*Sasha Sullivan*

A new kitten is like a time bomb of unexpected, unimaginable, friendly trouble. —*Murphy Malloy Kall*

Cats are endless opportunities for revelation.
—*Leslie Flanagan Kapp*

All little boys should have a cat so that they're not so stunned and unprepared when they grow up and meet a real woman.
—*Murphy Malloy Kall*

ACTION

Things do not happen. They are made to happen.
—*John F. Kennedy*

Inaction may be the highest form of action. —*Jerry Brown*

Is it really so difficult to tell a good action from a bad one? I think one usually knows right away or a moment afterward, in a horrid flash of regret. —*Mary McCarthy*

Love is a verb. —*Merrit Malloy*

What you can't get out of, get into wholeheartedly.
—*Mignon McLaughlin*

LIFE

Life is not for everyone. —*Michael O'Donoghue*

Life is for each man a solitary cell whose walls are mirrors.
—*Eugene O'Neill*

Life, for all its agonies of despair and loss and guilt, is exciting and beautiful, amusing and artful and endearing, full of liking and love, at times a poem and a high adventure, at times noble and at times very gay; and whatever (if anything) is to come after it—we shall not have this life again.　　*—Rose Macaulay*

Life is a learning process and you have to try to learn what's best for you. Let me tell you, life is not fun when you're banging your head against a brick wall all the time.　*—John McEnroe*

It's true that the Irish have a "certain something" and so too do the blacks—and also the Jews. What it is I cannot say in words, except to say it moves from within and its called *life*.
—Charlie Malloy

There comes a time in every man's life, and I've had plenty of them.　　　　　　　　　　　　　　　*—Casey Stengel*

LAST WORDS/EPITAPHS/ ENDINGS

Can we have a little travelling music? ... Aaaand A-WAY WE GO!!!　　　　　　　　　　　　　　*—Jackie Gleason*

Now will somebody give me a cigar?
—John Ford (reported as his last words)

Heee're's Johnny.　　　　　　　　　*—Ed McMahon*

I told you I was ill.　　*—Spike Milligan (self-written epitaph)*

Turn up the lights, I don't want to go home in the dark.
—O. Henry

This is my last slide.
—Michael J. "King" Kelly (remark attributed to the legendary baseball player when he fell off a stretcher during his last illness.)

You don't realize that what I'm doing here is the last tired effort of a man who once did something finer and better.
—F. Scott Fitzgerald

He finished the long trek alone.
—Anthony Quinn (his epitaph as he would write it)

I've played everything but a harp.　　*—Lionel Barrymore*

Thank Heavens the sun has gone in, and I don't have to go out and enjoy it. —*Logan Pearsall Smith*

Thank you, sister. May you be the mother of a bishop.
—*Brendan Behan (said to a nun on his deathbed)*

How were the receipts today in Madison Square Garden?
—*Phineas Taylor Barnum*

I let down my friends. I let down my country. I let down our system of government. —*Richard Nixon (May 1977)*

I have spent a lot of time searching through the Bible for loopholes. —*W. C. Fields*

You can keep the things of bronze and stone and give me one man to remember me just once a year. —*Damon Runyon*

You won't have Nixon to kick around any more, gentlemen. This is my last press conference.
—*Richard Nixon (after losing the California gubernatorial election, November 2, 1962)*

It's always a beautiful day in this neighborhood.
—*Fred Rogers (Mr. Rogers himself—epitaph in his own words)*

Surely there must be better gifts God could have given us than life. —*Michael O'Donoghue (as he would say it for himself)*

All in all, it's better than being in Philadelphia. —*W. C. Fields*

When the last dime is gone, I'll sit on the curb outside with a pencil and a ten-cent notebook and start the whole thing all over again. —*Preston Sturges*

It wouldn't be like I'm retired. It would be … a kind of fade-out. —*Jack Nicholson*

Captain, it is I—Ensign Pulver—and I just threw your stinking palm tree overboard. Now, what's all this crud about no movie tonight?
—*Jack Lemmon (standing up to James Cagney, in "Mr. Roberts")*

I'll be right back. —*Johnny Carson*

He was an average guy who could carry a tune.

> —*Bing Crosby (his epitaph, as he envisaged it)*

When I drove through the studio gate and the thrill was gone, I knew it was time to quit. —*Jimmy Cagney*

Any human life is as unimportant to the scheme of things as any single grain of sand is to the Sahara. At least, that's what I believe. I don't know what you want to do with your life, but I intend to enjoy mine. —*Gardner Mulloy*

COURAGE

Way down deep, we're all motivated by the same urges. Cats have the courage to live by them. —*Jim Davis*

One of the marks of a gift is to have the courage of it (also the talent). —*Katherine Anne Porter*

It isn't for the moment you are stuck that you need courage, but for the long uphill climb back to sanity and faith and security. —*Anne Morrow Lindbergh*

If you are brave too often, people will come to expect it of you. —*Mignon McLaughlin*

Lou Gehrig represents many things that are good in our society. He was famous for his unfortunate demise, for the way he faced his disease. —*Michael McCabe*

I thought it was all so much tomfoolery and humbug. That was at first. But I found that the most pious of them were the very bravest—and that astonished me more than anything. I saw these men tried in every way that men could be tried, and I never saw anything superior to them.

> —*John F. Maguire (of American soldiers)*

By not coming forward (about rape), you make yourself a victim forever. —*Kelly McGillis*

The only courage that matters is the kind that gets you from one minute to the next. —*Mignon McLaughlin*

Let your courage guide your future. —*Finlay McKenna*

Even cowards can endure hardship; only the brave can endure suspense. —*Mignon McLaughlin*

POVERTY

The poor are there to scare the **** out of the middle class.
—*George Carlin*

You don't seem to realize that a poor person who is unhappy is in a better position than a rich person who is unhappy. Because the poor person has hope. He thinks money would help. —*Jean Kerr*

The only advantage of being poor and in trouble is that your lawyer is free and is therefore worth every penny you've given to him. —*Pete Ferguson*

We were poor when I was young, but the difference then was the government didn't come around telling you you were poor. —*Ronald Reagan*

THAT WAY WITH WORDS

That's not a lie; it's a terminological inexactitude.
—*Alexander Haig*

A tie is like kissing your sister. —*Duffy Daugherty*

I'll have a pie à la mode with ice cream. —*John Logan*

The sun don't shine on the same dog's butt every day.
—*Babe McCarthy*

So what if they're taller—we'll play big.
—*George Ireland (basketball coach for Loyola of Chicago)*

I want to thank all my players for giving me the honor of being what I was. —*Casey Stengel*

We had to prick this boil and take the heat. Now that's what we are doing here. We're going to prick this boil and take the heat. —*Richard Nixon (from the Watergate transcripts)*

A habit of debt is very injurious to the memory.
—*Austin O'Malley*

You two-timed me one time too often.   —*Tex Ritter*

REAL LIFE

I was born in 1957. I have a wife, a child, a mortgage, two dogs, and gum disease.   —*Dave Barry*

When you don't have any money, the problem is food. When you have money, it's sex. When you have both, it's health. If everything is simply jake, then you're frightened of death.

—*J. P. Donleavy*

I know that when you teach somebody to drive, or give them a car, you give them wings. They may fly. That's part of the danger of life.   —*Jack Nicholson*

Time diminishes ... emotion ... and I came to realize that hometown and a home are different things. The former is an accident, usually unfortunate; the latter is a goal, frequently unattainable.   —*Larry McMurtry*

I find that most people know what a story is until they sit down to write one.   —*Flannery O'Connor*

Life is perhaps most wisely regarded as a bad dream between two awakenings, and every day is a life in miniature.

—*Eugene O'Neill*

Tomorrow is the most important thing in life. It comes into us at midnight very clean. It's perfect when it arrives, and it puts itself in our hands. It hopes we've learned something from yesterday.   —*John Wayne*

Faults shared are comfortable as bedroom slippers and as easy to slip into.   —*Phyllis McGinley*

Fretting about things you cannot do anything about creates more frustration than any other single factor. I believe that it can be a forerunner and a contributor to ulcers, high blood pressure, and similar disorders. ... If you try to reason with things you cannot do anything about, you are lost. Save your energy and your sanity by doing something on those matters that have an answer.   —*Ralph W. O'Farrell*

Life's under no obligation to give us what we expect. We take what we get and are thankful it's no worse than it is.

—Margaret Mitchell

The average, healthy, well-adjusted adult gets up at seven-thirty in the morning feeling just plain terrible.   *—Jean Kerr*

Coexistence is what the farmer does with the turkey until Thanksgiving.   *—Mike Connolly*

It's not the legs that go first—it's the hair.

—Pat Leahy (former New York Jets player
on being a 40–year-old place kicker)

Compromise? Of course, we compromise. But compromise, if not the spice of life, is its solidity. It is what makes nations great and marriages happy and ... [our house] the pleasant place it is.   *—Phyllis McGinley*

My life is composed of random, tangential, disparate episodes. Five wives; many liaisons, some more memorable than marriages. The hunting. The betting. The thoroughbreds. Painting, collecting. Boxing. Writing, directing, and acting in more than sixty pictures.   *—John Huston*

I knew that people could be mean, but I didn't realize how mean.   *—Drew Barrymore*

They call you a bum before you get to be champion. They call you a bum after somebody slaps you out of the title. And even while you're a champion, you're called a bum.   *—Jack Dempsey*

The first thing you have to do after suffering a stroke is to tell yourself you won't give up, that you don't want to die, or be cared for like a baby for the rest of your life. ... Now I'm healthy and have only a slight limp and some trouble remembering the names of people and places. But I get better every year, and I'm still working.   *—Patricia Neal*

The mass of men live lives of quiet exasperation. *—Phyllis McGinley*

People don't ever seem to realize that doing what's right's no guarantee against misfortune.   *—William McFee*

Life just is. You have to flow with it. Give yourself to the moment. Let it happen. —*Jerry Brown*

To understand it [life], to love it, to make it a little better, and to accept its buffetings as best we can and swim against them, knowing that we swim on and out toward a horizon we can never reach—this is all we can do. —*James T. Farrell*

I work mornings only. I go out to lunch. Afternoons I play with the baby, walk with my husband, or shovel mail. —*Annie Dillard*

If it isn't the sheriff, it's the finance company. I've got more attachments on me than a vacuum cleaner. —*John Barrymore*

He dreamed he was eating shredded wheat and woke up to find the mattress half gone. —*Fred Allen*

Nobody owes anybody a living, but everybody is entitled to a chance. —*Jack Dempsey*

NOTES FROM THE PROS

Learn your lines and don't bump into the furniture.
—*Spencer Tracy*

I always preferred a running offense, but I was smart enough to put in one long incomplete pass per quarter just for the alumni. —*Duffy Daugherty*

Hold when you're at home and don't hold when you're on the road. —*John McKay (U.S.C. football coach)*

You do not create a style. You work and develop yourself; your style is an emanation from your own being.
—*Katherine Anne Porter*

The writer should never be ashamed of staring. There is nothing that does not require his attention. —*Flannery O'Connor*

How much it takes to become a writer. Bent (far more common than we assume) circumstances, time, development of craft—but beyond that: how much conviction as to the importance of what one has to say, one's right to say it. —*Tillie Olson*

Watch what we do, not what we say. —*John Mitchell*

Look at your choices, pick the best one, then go with it.

—*Pat Riley*

You need four things to even have a chance in this music business. To start with, you need the dream, the desire to burn bright. You need the talent to back up that dream and the guts to be true to yourself about it. And you need persistence. ... But the fourth and most important thing is that you need to be blind, deaf, and dumb. —*Eddie Rabbit*

It may be that the race is not always to the swift, nor the battle to the strong—but that is the way to bet. —*Damon Runyon*

Surround yourself with the best people you can find, delegate authority, and don't interfere. —*Ronald Reagan*

A lot of what acting is, is paying attention. —*Robert Redford*

MEN

It's always the mind with me—I don't care if the guy looks like a bowling ball. —*Shirley MacLaine*

When a man brings his wife flowers for no reason—there's a reason. —*Molly McGee*

Men may be allowed romanticism; women, who can create life in their own bodies, dare not indulge in it. —*Phyllis McGinley*

I don't need a man to rectify my existence. The most profound relationship we'll ever have is the one with ourselves.

—*Shirley MacLaine*

Men say they love independence in a woman, but they don't waste a second demolishing it brick by brick. —*Candice Bergen*

Women speak because they wish to speak, whereas a man speaks only when driven to speech by something outside himself—like, for instance, he can't find any clean socks. —*Jean Kerr*

I get bored with a man who isn't emotionally conversant with himself. —*Shirley MacLaine*

Money

Money hasn't really been the issue for me for quite a while. I just do what I feel like—that's all there is to do. —*Jack Nicholson*

Money may not be everything, but it does buy fresh cat litter.
—*Mac (Malloy) Wiest*

We're fighting for only one thing—money. —*Sid Flaherty (boxer)*

We have come to know what things cost and not what they mean. We have come to measure our lives in what we can afford to buy rather than in what we can't afford to lose. Value is what we miss about money. —*Merrit Malloy*

Money: in its absence we are coarse; in its presence we are vulgar. —*Mignon McLaughlin*

There are a handful of people whom money won't spoil, and we count ourselves among them. —*Mignon McLaughlin*

It's extraordinary how many emotional storms one may weather in safety if one is ballasted with ever so little gold. —*William McFee*

Leadership/Instinct

If a manager of mine ever said someone was indispensable, I'd fire him. —*Charley Finley (owner of the Oakland A's)*

I'm a commercial writer, not an "author." Margaret Mitchell was an author. She wrote one book. —*Mickey Spillane*

Results

The world is not interested in the storms you encountered, but did you bring in the ship? —*William McFee*

Cats are God's way of showing us that results are not as important as we think. —*Merrit Malloy*

Passion

It's useless to try to hold someone to anything they say while they're madly in love, drunk, or running for office.
—*E. C. McKenzie*

Great stories are emotional and not intellectual.   —*Bob McKee*

Baseball isn't a business, it's more like a disease.
—*Walter O'Malley*

That's what everybody works to find: the unfair advantage.
—*Mark Donohue (late race car driver on his newly designed car.)*

THEORY

If God had wanted cats to run the world, we would have had Maxie and Whiskers instead of Adam and Eve. We still would have had "original sin" however—only it would have been called "Whoopie."   —*Nan "Swifty" Porter*

It was not the apple on the tree, but the pair on the ground, I believe, that caused the trouble in the garden.
—*M. D. O'Connor*

RELIGION/FAITH

We have no right to reconstruct (Christianity) as we like or choose. We are not authorized to change Our Father into Our Mother.   —*Cardinal John J. O'Connor*

The hardest thing for me to believe about the Bible is that there were only two asses on Noah's Ark.   —*Larry Wilde*

Some people are willing to serve God, but only as his consultant.   —*E. C. McKenzie*

Catholicism has changed tremendously in recent years. Now when Communion is served, there is also a salad bar.
—*Bill Maher*

My husband is Jewish and I'm Irish Catholic. We've decided to raise our children Jewish, but I get to pick the names—Mary Magdalene and Sean Patrick.   —*Jeannie McBride*

When the game is on Ash Wednesday and the ref shows up with a smudge on his forehead, I know I'm in trouble.
—*Jack McCloskey (Wake Forest basketball coach, after losing to St. Joseph's)*

The atheist can't find God for the same reason that a thief can't find a policeman. —*E. C. McKenzie*

For the wonderful thing about saints is that they were human. They lost their tempers, got hungry, scolded God, were egotistical or testy or impatient in their turns, made mistakes and regretted them. Still they went on doggedly blundering toward heaven. —*Phyllis McGinley*

There is an advantage to being half Catholic and half Jewish. You still have to go to confession, but you can bring your lawyer. —*Ed Mann*

I don't know whether you have any rights before you're born. All I know is that being born again doesn't entitle you to twice as many. —*A. Whitney Brown*

Do we really deserve top billing?
—*Fred Allen (on a meeting of the National Conference of Christians and Jews)*

As you all know, some circles have invented the myth that after Al Smith's defeat in 1928, he sent a one-word telegram to the pope: "Unpack!" After my press conference on the school bill [which included no mention of aid to parochial schools], I received a one-word wire from the pope: "Pack!" —*John F. Kennedy*

My uncle got a job driving a cab. He had the cab parked right in front of Grand Central Station, and an Episcopal bishop got into my uncle's cab. He said, "Take me to Christ Church." So my uncle took him up to St. Patrick's Cathedral. And the bishop got mad. He said, "I said Christ Church." And my uncle said "Look, if he's not here, he's not in town." —*Jimmy Joyce*

I don't care what religion he is. If he doesn't get moving, he's gonna lose the fight.
—*Gil Clancy (announcer, after being told a boxer was a vegetarian.)*

A few Catholics have criticized me because of my assurances that, as president, I would not be influenced by the Vatican. Now I can understand why Henry the Eighth set up his own church. —*John F. Kennedy*

A priest I know has presided at so many shotgun weddings, he renamed his church Winchester Cathedral.   —*Larry Wilde*

Madam, this is not an easy question. All I can say is that a few months ago in Rome His Holiness called me "Jibbons."
> —*James Cardinal Gibbons (on whether the*
> *pope and papal doctrine are infallible.)*

Yes, I have doubted, I have wandered off the path, I have been lost. But I have always returned. It is beyond the logic I seek. It is intuitive—an intrinsic, built-in sense of direction. I seem always to find my way home. My faith has wavered but has saved me.   —*Helen Hayes*

I grew up Catholic, which is good, because it gives you something to work out the rest of your life.   —*Steve Sweeney*

IRISH GUILT

I was liberated, but not too liberated. I was Catholic, you see, and my conscience bothered me.   —*Eileen O'Casey*

Every time I see a cop, I turn myself in. —*Stephen York O'Donnell*

Cats remember everything. This is why we always lock them out of the room when we call in sick.   —*H. Thomas (Collins) Yu*

CHARITY

I get fifteen or twenty letters a day for everything from Yugoslavian dog illnesses to marathon diseases. It numbs you. ... So you write off a check for twenty dollars to a charity to absolve yourself of guilt.   —*Anjelica Huston*

Honey, when it comes to charity, the Catholics take the cake.
—*Grace Boyle*

We live in the century of the Appeal. ... One applauds the industry of professional philanthropy. But it has its dangers. After a while the private heart begins to harden. We fling letters into the wastebasket, are abrupt to telephone solicitations. Charity withers in the incessant gale.   —*Phyllis McGinley*

PRIORITIES

I spent ninety percent of my salary on good Irish whiskey and women. The rest I wasted.
—*Tug McGraw*

It's silly talking about how many years we will have to spend in the jungles of Vietnam when we could pave the whole country and put parking stripes on it and still be home for Christmas.
—*Ronald Reagan*

No one works till the writer works.
—*Robert McKee*

It is, of course, totally pointless to call a cat when it is intent on the chase. They are deaf to the interruptive nonsense of humans. They are on cat business, totally serious and involved.
—*John D. MacDonald*

As far as I can tell, the only healthy attitude for a writer is to consider praise, blame, book chat, and table position at Elaine's irrelevant to writing, and to get on with it.
—*Jay McInerney*

I spend just the right amount of time on my hair. I'm trying to achieve something between Pee Wee Herman and Mel Gibson.
—*Bob McGrath (Sesame Street regular)*

IRISH LOGIC/IRISHISMS

You can get more with a kind word and a gun than you can with a kind word alone.
—*Johnny Carson*

A house is a place to keep your stuff while you go out and get *more* stuff.
—*George Carlin*

Smoking kills. If you're killed, you've lost a very important part of your life.
—*Brooke Shields*

About all that losing gracefully can teach a boy is how to lose.
—*James Kelly*

Half the game (hockey) is mental; the other half is being mental.
—*Jim McKenny*

It is the wallop that wins.
—*Jimmy Wilde*

I can't rationalize talking to press people, because they're not rational people. —*John McEnroe*

If the waitress has dirty ankles, the chili should be good.
—*Al McGuire*

Never bet on a dead horse or a live woman. Never play cards with a man with dark glasses or his own deck. —*Jim Murray*

Isn't it just like Jesus to be born on Christmas morning?
—*Merrit Malloy*

All right, everyone—line up alphabetically according to your height. —*Casey Stengel*

I like it [his '54 Buick] because it plays old music.
—*Tug McGraw*

What you're looking for is looking for you, too. —*Merrit Malloy*

DOCTORS/MEDICINE

I hope you are all Republicans. —*Ronald Reagan (to his surgeons)*

I'm going to Boston to see my doctor. He's a very sick man.
—*Fred Allen*

Patient to doctor: "But if I'm a hypochondriac, how will I know when I really do get sick?" —*McCotic (cartoonist)*

Remember, half the doctors in the country graduated in the bottom half of their class. —*Al McGuire*

When I was in high school the worst thing you could get was V.D.. Talk about the sniffles! I just want to meet an old-fashioned girl with gonorrhea. —*Bill Maher*

A hospital should also have a recovery room adjoining the cashier's office. —*Francis O'Walsh*

A psychiatrist is the next man you start talking to after you start talking to yourself. —*Fred Allen*

Psychoanalysis is spending forty dollars an hour to squeal on your mother. —*Mike Connolly*

The doctors X-rayed my head and found nothing. —*Dizzy Dean*

The trouble with doctors is not that they don't know enough, but that they don't see enough. —*Sir Dominic J. Corrigan*

IRONY

The two biggest sellers in any bookstore are the cookbooks and the diet books. The cookbooks tell you how to prepare the food, and the diet books tell you how not to eat any of it.

—*Andy Rooney*

The bigger they are, the harder they fall. —*John L. Sullivan*

When we make up our minds, we close them.

—*Shauna Sorensen*

The maximum amount of seriousness admits the maximum amount of comedy. —*Flannery O'Connor*

You get your teeth fixed, your mouth doesn't work.

Bridget O'Donnell

How ironic that the fatal flaw of communism would turn out to be that there is no money in it. —*A. Whitney Brown*

If there's anything I hate, it's a bully. —*Jack Dempsey*

I don't approve of people talking about their private lives.

—*Diane Keaton*

One cannot collect all the beautiful shells on the beach. One can collect only a few, and they are more beautiful if they are few. —*Anne Morrow Lindbergh*

I have hair and yet I'm bald. —*Bob Nickman*

Crisis has become a banality. —*Frank Murphy*

If it weren't for bad news, we wouldn't have news at all.

—*James R. Peterson*

COMPETITION

If a man is sexy, that doesn't offend the men in the crowd. They know the women are just having fun. But if a gal is sexy and something of a come-on, the women in the audience take offense. They don't want their husbands or their boyfriends seeing that. —*Reba McEntire*

Right now, ten percent of the baseball players are making all the money. The rest are jealous. —*Joe Burke*

Winning is better than losing. —*John F. (John-John) Kennedy Jr.*

Victory has a hundred fathers, but defeat is an orphan.
—*John F. Kennedy*

One night we play like King Kong, the next night we play like Fay Wray. —*Terry Kennedy, (catcher for the San Diego Padres)*

THE EXAMINED LIFE

I'm a nut, but not *just* a nut. —*Bill Murray*

The world is a mystery. There are mysteries on all sides of us. And the beginning of the mystery of life is the mystery of ourselves. Along with the mystery of ourselves, there is the mystery of other people. We don't know ourselves too well, and we don't know other people very well. Novels in which there is some kind of truth help us to explore the mystery, help to give us the feeling that life is a little less mysterious, that life is a little less awesome and fearful. —*James T. Farrell*

By nature, I am not monogamous. —*Jack Nicholson*

Loving you is how I recognize myself. —*Merrit Malloy*

It all starts with self-reflection. Then you can know and empathize more profoundly with someone else. —*Shirley MacLaine*

We must get in touch with our own liberating ludicrousness and practice being harmlessly deviant. —*Sarah J. McCarthy*

Self-evaluation. It is the skin rash of the emotionally insecure.
—*John D. MacDonald*

I think I'm really not interested in the quest for the self anymore. It's absolutely useless to look for it, you won't find it, but it's possible in some sense to make it. —*Mary McCarthy*

The moment you believe your own hype, your growth stops.
—*Patrick Swayze*

I feel there is something unexplored about women that only a woman can explore. —*Georgia O'Keeffe*

PHILOSOPHY

What you choose has to do with who you are. —*Jack Nicholson*

I believe in having a little fight in most everything except funerals. —*John L. Sullivan*

The person who knows how to laugh at himself will never cease to be amused. —*Shirley MacLaine*

Have a day. —*Merrit Malloy*

If you jot down every silly thought that pops into your mind, you will soon find out everything you most seriously believe.
—*Mignon McLaughlin*

There's right and there's wrong. You get to do one or the other. You do the one, and you're living. You do the other, and you may be walking around, but you're dead as a beaver hat.
—*John Wayne*

I don't deal with yesterday, and I don't fear tomorrow. But I deal with today with as much energy as I can summon!
—*Jack Nicholson*

I think I am, therefore I am, I think.
—*M. M. Malloy* (Sister Mary Tricky [Penguin] in cartoon)

Nothing is impossible for the person who doesn't have to do it.
—*Murphy's Law #4002*

FOREIGNERS

These people [the Japanese] have been fighting for 5,000 years, and they can't even agree on what year it is. —*A. Whitney Brown*

The Soviet bureaucracy is about as efficient as a Mexican traffic court that doesn't take bribes. All they need is crack, and Russia would be as bad as the Bronx. —*A. Whitney Brown*

I am a Berliner.
                                                    —*John F. Kennedy*

Even the Canadians, with all their separatist squabbles, share the powerful bond that, one and all, they aren't Americans, eh?   —*A. Whitney Brown*

NATURE/ENVIRONMENT

If you've seen one redwood, you've seen them all.
                                                    —*Ronald Reagan*

The people most affected by environmental policy aren't born yet.   —*Robert F. Kennedy Jr.*

Plant trees. They give us two of the most crucial elements for our survival: oxygen and books.   —*A. Whitney Brown*

Cats are nature's way of teaching us patience.
                                            —*Molly (Malloy) Wiest*

Other people have analysis, I have Utah.   —*Robert Redford*

Today my mind resembles a Venus flytrap, always poised and ready. If a gag even comes close, I snap shut on it and I exclude nothing.   —*John Callahan*

THE LUCK OF THE IRISH

If you're lucky enough to be Irish, you're lucky enough.
                                                    —*Grace Boyle*

Your luck is how you treat people.   —*Bridget O'Donnell*

I'd like to be lucky enough so that I could throw the soap away after the letters are worn off.   —*Andy Rooney*

Having Marv Throneberry play for your team is like having Willie Sutton play for your bank.   —*Jimmy Breslin*

Politics is an astonishing profession. It has enabled me to go from being an obscure member of the junior varsity at Harvard to being an honorary member of the Football Hall of Fame.   —*John F. Kennedy*

THE PRESS

The big print giveth and the small print taketh away.

—*Bishop Fulton Sheen*

If you think the football game was exciting, wait until you hear the report from Tom Aspell from Amman, Jordan.

—*Tom Brokaw (lead in to news)*

All I've been asked by the press … is about a woman I didn't sleep with and a draft I didn't dodge.   —*Bill Clinton*

Bad press put me where I am. If they didn't write about me at all, I wouldn't be famous.   —*Delta Burke*

Karl Marx wrote for the Herald Tribune, but that is not why I cancelled my subscription.   —*John F. Kennedy*

If there had been a Jim Murray when I was [playing football] at Eureka College, I might have had a successful career—and become famous. Instead, I ended up in Washington for eight years in public housing.   —*Ronald Reagan*

Writers like to say they've seen a lot of players come and go. I've seen a lot of writers come and go.   —*Nolan Ryan*

HISTORY

History is bunk.   —*Henry Ford*

History is gossip.   —*John F. Kennedy*

In ancient times, they sacrificed virgins. Men were not about to sacrifice the sluts.   —*Bill Maher*

History must always be taken with a grain of salt. It is, after all, not a science but an art. …   —*Phyllis McGinley*

Current events, as we shall see, are nothing more than a teeming school of red herring in the vast sea of history, clogging the nets of those who strain for the truth.   —*A. Whitney Brown*

History is a very tricky thing. To begin with, you can't get it mixed up with the past. The past actually happened, but history is only what someone wrote down.   —*A. Whitney Brown*

History teaches that wars begin when governments believe the price of aggression is cheap. —*Ronald Reagan*

The greatest battle in American history was the Battle of the Little Big Horn. The Indians wiped out the white men, scalped them. That was a victory in American history. It should be featured in all our schoolbooks as the greatest victory in American history. —*Eugene O'Neill*

"Henry," I said, "we've done it." I said: "Remember Lot's wife. Never look back." I don't know whether Henry [Kissinger] had read the Old Testament or not, but I had, and he got the point. Henry and I often had a little joke between us after that. Whenever he would come in and say, "Well, I'm not sure we should have done this, or that, or the other thing," I would say, "Henry, remember Lot's wife." And that would end the conversation. —*Richard Nixon*

THE SHARP-TONGUED

Nixon is a purposeless man, but I have great faith in his cowardice. —*Jimmy Breslin*

Phyllis Schlafly speaks for all American women who oppose equal rights for themselves. —*Andy Rooney*

Elsa Lanchester looks as though butter wouldn't melt in her mouth, or anywhere else. —*Maureen O'Hara*

You gotta live somewhere.
—*Jimmy Brogan (possible motto for Cleveland)*

I like long walks, especially when they are taken by people who annoy me. —*Fred Allen*

Some of these people would boo the crack in the Liberty Bell.
—*Pete Rose (on Philadelphia fans)*

Condolences to Beth Daniel, who pulled out of the LPGA deMaurier Classic because her dog died. I know. I couldn't believe it either. —*Dan McGrath*

The reason there are so few female politicians is that it is too much trouble to put makeup on two faces. —*Maureen Murphy*

Why don't we talk about this Monday when you pick up my trash?

—*Sean Farrell (Tampa Bay Buccaneers guard to a heckling fan)*

Story talent is rare and unconnected to literary talent, which is common. —*Bob McKee*

What's on your mind, if you will allow the overstatement?

—*Fred Allen*

When Charlie Finley had his heart operation, it took eight hours—seven just to find his heart. —*Steve McCatty*

If a contest had 97 prizes, the 98th would be a trip to Green Bay. —*John McKay*

APPROVAL

They gave me a standing observation.

—*Bill Peterson, (Florida State coach)*

I don't try to guess what a million people will like. It's hard enough to know what I like. —*John Huston*

There's something about me that makes a lot of people want to throw up. —*Pat Boone*

Appeasers believe that if you keep throwing steaks to a tiger, the tiger will become a vegetarian. —*Heywood Broun*

It was about three to one that I was not an S.O.B. But there were a lot of ones.

—*John McKay (on "fan mail" received as the Tampa Bay coach)*

I enjoy the oohs and aahs from the gallery when I hit my drives. But I'm getting pretty tired of the awws and uhhs when I miss the putt. —*Jack Nicklaus*

THE IRISH EGO

I am in control here. As of now, I am in control here at the White House. —*Alexander Haig (as secretary of state, after President Reagan was shot, 1981)*

I would have made a good pope. —*Richard Nixon*

I want my Hamlet to be so masculine that when I come out on stage, they can hear my balls clank! —*John Barrymore*

The last time I saw him, he was walking down Lover's Lane holding his own hand. —*Fred Allen*

I happened to catch my reflection the other day when I was polishing my trophies, and, gee, it's easy to see why women are nuts about me. —*Tom Ryan*

If Thomas Wolfe sold, I'd write like Thomas Wolfe.
—*Mickey Spillane*

I'm the most translated writer in the world, behind Lenin, Tolstoy, Gorki, and Jules Verne. And they're all dead.
—*Mickey Spillane*

Me. —*Duffy Daugherty (when asked who he was happiest to see return to Michigan State)*

Irish is English set to music. —*Mary Michael Malloy*

EXAGGERATION

This is the greatest week in the history of the world since the creation. —*Richard Nixon (of the moon landing, July 24, 1969)*

Only Thomas Edison could invent a course Washburn could pass. —*Jim Murray (on Chris Washburn's acceptance to North Carolina State with an SAT score of 470)*

At vast expense, the ambassadors offer up their livers almost every night in the service of their country. —*Patrick O'Donovan*

I managed a team that was so bad, we considered a 2-and-0 count on the batter a rally. —*Rich Donnelly*

Mary, you're so skinny—if you drank tomato juice you'd look like a thermometer. —*Bridget O'Donnell*

GROWING UP

I was raised by just my mom. See, my father died when I was eight years old. At least, that's what he told us in the letter.
—*Drew Carey*

I went straight from shenanigans to crimes against humanity.

—*George Carlin*

One has to grow up with good talk in order to form the habit of it.

—*Helen Hayes*

I was a loner as a child. I had an imaginary friend—I didn't bother with him.

—*George Carlin*

One hears one's childhood and it is ancient.

—*Kathleen Fraser*

There are more bores around than when I was a boy.

—*Fred Allen*

If the F.B.I. went back far enough, I was always suspect: I never liked football.

—*Daniel Berrigan*

I was 40 when I was 16.

—*Bill Clinton*

Strategy

I'd get real close to him and breathe on his goggles.

—*Johnny Kerr (on how he'd handle Kareem Abdul-Jabbar)*

When you're getting kicked from the rear, it means you're in front.

—*Bishop Fulton Sheen*

Keep the villain chasing the girl.

—*Randall Miller (saxophone player)*

It's better to be quiet and ignorant than to open your mouth and remove all doubt.

—*John McNamara*

The Irish Wit

She was just a passing fiancée.

—*Alfred McFote*

Yes, I am Frank Sinatra's love child, I admit it. I guess he did it his way.

—*Ronald (Ron) Reagan Jr.*

Treat people as equals, and the first thing you know they believe they are.

—*James Mulligan (one businessman to another; from a cartoon in The New Yorker)*

I don't know. I never smoked AstroTurf.

—*Tug McGraw (on whether he favored real or artificial grass)*

No, ma'am. I was a jockey for a dinosaur.

> —*Johnny Kerr (response to being asked whether
> the 6'9" man had ever played basketball)*

Look, show me something for about $300 from a sheep that's fooled around a little.

> —*Chuck Daly (after being offered a $1,300 virgin wool suit)*

Eliminate the referees, raise the basket four feet, double the size of the basketball, limit the height of the players to 5'9", bring back the center jump, allow taxi drivers in free, and allow the players to carry guns.

> —*Al McGuire (on how to make basketball more exciting)*

Yeah, Will Rogers.

> —*Joe Don Looney (when asked if he'd ever met a man he didn't like)*

I think this is the most extraordinary collection of talent, of human knowledge, that has ever been gathered together at the White House, with the possible exception of when Thomas Jefferson dined alone.

> —*John F. Kennedy (at a dinner for Nobel prizewinners, 1962)*

I wish I were Adam. That way when I told a joke, no one could say, "Oh, I heard that one already."   —*Larry Wilde*

George [Burns], just the other night, I thought Nancy had one of your records on. It turned out to be a spoon caught in the garbage disposal.   —*Ronald Reagan (at George Burns' roast)*

Wit is not the prerogative of the unjust, and there is truly laughter in holy places.   —*Phyllis McGinley*

WHAT COUNTS

Your name and your word are it.   —*Bob McKinzie (truck driver)*

Where and when I was born and where and how I have lived is unimportant. It is what I have done with where I have been that should be of interest.   —*Georgia O'Keeffe*

You usually wind up staying up all night until your best player comes in.   —*John McCay (on the uselessness of enforcing curfews)*

Show me a man who plays a good game of golf, and I'll show you a man who's neglecting something.   —*John F. Kennedy*

If you don't do a ✳✳✳✳ thing but stand there and look at your kid, it takes you up, way up. Look, having a baby is very big. You don't want to make people envious or anything, but it overwhelms. Everything else is peanuts.   —*Jack Nicholson*

The more you strive to be sensible and serious and meaningful, the less chance you have of becoming so. The primary objective is to laugh.   —*John D. MacDonald*

It's no sin to sell dear; but a sin to give ill measure.

—*James Kelley*

First you have to know how to do what you want to do with a particular song. Then there's the next step, which is turning the song into your own.   —*Judy Collins*

ACCOLADES/HONORS

I don't know about you, but winning a Grammy sure helped me get laid.   —*Bonnie Raitt*

Every society honors its live conformists and its dead trouble-makers.   —*Mignon McLaughlin*

People who become legends in their own time usually have very little time left.   —*John D. MacDonald*

He writes so well he makes me feel like putting my quill back in my goose.   —*Fred Allen*

Nobody there to share your triumph? Do not despair, reach your arm above your head, bend it at the elbow and pat yourself on the back saying all the while "Job well done."

—*Finlay McKenna*

THE RULES OF THE GAME

Let me tell you about boxing. It's the most treacherous, dirtiest, vicious, cheatingest game in the world. That's the nature of the business.   —*Paddy Flood*

If a pitcher feels he has been intimidated by a hitter, he has a right to throw at him.   *—Lane McGlothen*

FAME AND FORTUNE

If you could give up fame and keep the fortune, you could go on with your life and keep going to Wal-Mart and keep spending money. And nobody would know who you are. That would be pretty darn good.   *—Reba McEntire*

I get a kick out of movie stars.   *—Jack Nicholson*

How much fame, money, and power does a woman have to achieve on her own before you can punch her in the face?
—P. J. O'Rourke

As much as you try to be a regular guy, you can't.
—Robert Redford

Show me a hero, and I will write you a tragedy.
—F. Scott Fitzgerald

You wonder about people who made a fortune, and you always think they drank it up or stuck it up their nose. That's not usually what brings on the decline. It's usually the battle to keep your creative child alive while keeping your business shark alive. You have to develop cunning and shrewdness and other things which are well suited to the arts.   *—Joni Mitchell*

It's not very often you get to see the Lone Ranger and Toronto the same night.   *—Bobby Bragan (on the night his team played host to actor Clayton [The Lone Ranger] Moore, the same night his team played the Blue Jays)*

The world is as good as you are. You've got to learn to like yourself first. I'm a little screwed up, but I'm beautiful.
—Steve McQueen

COMPENSATION

Self-sacrifice is never entirely unselfish, for the giver never fails to receive.   *—Dolores E. McGuire*

I work well on praise.   *—Finlay McKenna*

We [the Oklahoma State Penitentiary basketball team] lost some mighty good players from last year because of paroles, but, crime being what it is, we've picked up some good ones since then, too. —*Joe Kirkpatrick*

What you have become is the price you paid to get what you used to want. —*Mignon McLaughlin*

The freshmen bring a little knowledge in and the seniors take none out, so it accumulates over the years. —*A. Lowell*

If all else fails, immortality can always be assured by spectacular failure. —*John Kenneth Galbraith*

What lawyers lack in sensitivity, they make up in fees.
—*M. Malloy*

HUMAN BEHAVIOR

We are a very perverse, complex people. It's what makes us lovable. We're banking heavily that God has sense of humor.
—*Jim Murray*

My mind and body are going in the same direction but not at the same speed. —*Margaret Randall*

It's innocence when it charms us, ignorance when it doesn't.
—*Mignon McLaughlin*

I once knew a man who took off all his clothes and jumped in a mess of cactus. When I asked him why, he said, "It seemed like a good idea at the time." —*Steve McQueen*

Our strength is often composed of the weaknesses we're damned if we're going to show. —*Mignon McLaughlin*

It appears that every man's insomnia is as different from his neighbor's as are their daytime hopes and aspirations.
—*F. Scott Fitzgerald*

We are all born brave, trusting, and greedy, and most of us remain greedy. —*Mignon McLaughlin*

You are not tempted because you are evil; you are tempted because you are human. —*Bishop Fulton J. Sheen*

QUIPS AND QUOTABLES

Sheets can be kept clean by getting drunk and falling asleep with your clothes on. —*P. J. O'Rourke*

She didn't know it couldn't be done, so she went ahead and did it. —*Bridget O'Donnell*

Hearst come, Hearst served.
  —*Marion Davies (actress and mistress of William Randolph Hearst)*

All horseplayers die broke. —*Damon Runyon*

Why not go out on a limb? Isn't that where the fruit is?
—*Frank Scully*

Forgive your enemies, but never forget their names.
—*John F. Kennedy*

FRIENDSHIP

It's wonderful to meet so many friends I didn't use to like.
—*Casey Stengel*

Love forgives; friendship prorates. … Love invests; friendship speculates. … Love is unconditional; friendship has clauses.
—*James Collins*

No man can coach his buddies. —*Frank McGuire*

Wit … is, after all, a form of arousal. We challenge one another to be funnier and smarter. It's high-energy play. It's the way friends make love to one another. —*Anne Gottlieb*

THE BOYS OF SUMMER

If Jesus were on the field, he'd be pitching inside and breaking up double plays. —*Tim Burke*

I haven't missed a game in two-and-half years, I go to the park sick as a dog, and when I see my uniform hanging there, I get well right away. Then I see some of you [press] guys, and I get sick again. —*Pete Rose*

I think genetics plays the biggest role. —*Nolan Ryan*

Baseball is almost the only place where sacrifice is really appreciated. —*E. C. McKenzie*

None, really. But I never pitch well on days they play the national anthem.
—*Mike Flanagan (on whether he had any superstitions)*

You have to have a certain dullness of mind to play [baseball] here [Chicago]. I went through psychoanalysis and that helped me deal with my Cubness. —*Jim Brosnan*

I'll have to go with the immoral Babe Ruth.
—*Johnny Logan (on the best baseball player of all time.)*

WAR/MILITARY

The real war is on clichés. —*Robert McKee*

Right is more precious than peace. —*Woodrow Wilson*

Of the four wars in my lifetime, none came about because the United States was too strong. —*Ronald Reagan*

The troops will march in, the bands will play, the crowds will cheer, and in four days everyone will have forgotten. Then we will be told we have to send in more troops. It's like taking a drink. The effect wears off, and you have to take another.
—*John F. Kennedy*

Missiles will be able to do anything bombers can do—cheaper.
—*Robert McNamara*

A revolution is interesting insofar as it avoids like the plague the plague it promised to heal. —*Daniel Berrigan*

War will exist until that distant day when the conscientious objector enjoys the same reputation and prestige that the warrior does today. —*John F. Kennedy*

What the hell difference does it make, left or right? There were good men lost on both sides. —*Brendan Behan*

Everybody should rise up and say, "Thank you, Mr. President, for bombing Haiphong." —*Martha Mitchell (to a women's group)*

The more horrible a depersonalized scientific mass war becomes, the more necessary it is to find universal ideal motives to justify it.
—*John Dewey*

Wars frequently begin ten years before the first shot is fired.
—*K. K. V. Casey*

Ours was a picked lot. They came mainly from the Irish County Societies and the Catholic Athletic Clubs. A number of the latter bore distinctly German, French, Italian, or Polish names. They were Irish by adoption, Irish by association, or Irish by conviction.
—*Father Francis P. Duffy (chaplain of the World War I's legendary Fighting 69th)*

That's what went wrong with Vietnam ... we pulled out. Not very manly.
—*George Carlin*

If peace ... only had the music and pageantry of war, there'd be no wars.
—*Sophie Kerr*

EDUCATION

I think the world is run by C students.
—*Al McGuire*

The kids from 15 countries took math and science tests. We came in 14th, behind Slovenia, which has only been a country since Tuesday.
—*Bill Maher*

Everywhere I go I'm asked if I think the university stifles writers. My opinion is that they don't stifle enough of them.
—*Flannery O'Connor*

When I finished school I took one of those career aptitude tests and, based on my verbal ability score, they suggested I become a mime.
—*Tim Cavanaugh*

I'd have scored higher on my SAT but I was on steroids and kept breaking my pencil.
—*Cochran (cartoonist)*

I'm thirty years old but I read at the thirty-four-year level.
—*Dana Carvey (Canadian Irish descent)*

The book to read is not the one which thinks for you, but the one which makes you think.
—*James McCosh*

You've got to wonder about a country where the bombs are smarter than the high school graduates. At least the bombs can find Iraq on the world map. —*A. Whitney Brown*

Freedom

Liberty without learning is always in peril; learning without liberty is always in vain. —*John F. Kennedy*

What I am describing now is a plan and a hope for the long term—the march of freedom and democracy which will leave Marxism-Leninism on the ash heap of history as it has left other tyrannies which stifle the freedom and muzzle the self-expression of the people.
—*Ronald Reagan (addressing the British Parliament)*

Until you've lost your reputation, you never realize what a burden it was or what freedom really is. —*Margaret Mitchell*

The first step toward liberation for any group is to use the power in hand. … And the power in hand is the vote.
—*Helen Gahagan Douglas*

Those who make peaceful revolution impossible will make violent revolution inevitable. —*John F. Kennedy*

Comprehension

If you can keep your head when all about you are losing theirs, its possible you haven't grasped the situation. —*Jean Kerr*

"Love or perish" we are told and we tell ourselves. The phrase is true enough so long as we do not interpret it as "Mingle or be a failure." —*Phyllis McGinley*

There are no new truths, but only truths that have not been recognized by those who have perceived them without noticing. —*Mary McCarthy*

In film story, the truth isn't what happens, it's why it happens and how, and the meaning of all that together. —*Bob McKee*

Level with your children by being honest. Nobody spots a phony quicker than a child. —*Mary MacCracken*

Modern neurosis began with the discoveries of Copernicus. Science made man feel small by showing him that the earth was not the center of the universe. —*Mary McCarthy*

Man has no nobler function than to defend the truth.
—*Ruth McKenney*

Truth could never be wholly contained in words. ... At the same moment the mouth is speaking one thing, the heart is saying another. —*Catherine Marshall*

What loves does not wear out. —*Merrit Malloy*

CRITICS

Critics are like eunuchs in a harem. They're there every night, they see it done every night, they see how it should be done every night, but they can't do it themselves. —*Brendan Behan*

Many a critic seems more like a committee framing resolutions than a man writing down what he thinks.
—*Frank Moore Colby*

A critic is someone who never actually goes to the battle, yet who afterwards comes out shooting the wounded. —*Tyne Daly*

Confronted by an absolutely infuriating review, it is sometimes helpful for the victim to do a little personal research on the critic. Is there any truth to the rumor that he had no formal education beyond the age of eleven? In any event, is he able to construct a simple English sentence? Do his participles dangle? When moved to lyricism, does he write "I had a fun time"? Was he ever arrested for burglary? I don't know that you will prove anything this way, but it is perfectly harmless and quite soothing. —*Jean Kerr*

Book reviewers are little old ladies of both sexes. —*John O'Hara*

The critics have missed the most important thing about me and my work, the fact that I am Irish. —*Eugene O'Neill*

A book reviewer is usually a barker before the door of a publisher's circus. —*Austin O'Malley*

DREAMERS

We build our own myths. We live in the flatlands, and the myths are our mountains, so we build them to change the contours of our lives to make them more interesting.

—*John D. MacDonald*

The lie of a pipe dream is what gives life to the whole misbegotten mad lot of us, drunk or sober.   —*Eugene O'Neill*

Obsessed by a fairy tale, we spend our lives searching for a magic door and a lost kingdom of peace.   —*Eugene O'Neill*

TRAVEL

I had the chance to go to London a couple of months back. Had kind of a weird flight over there, though, 'cause one of the flight attendants got very angry with me. She said, "Sir, you really shouldn't waste all that food. There are people starving on Air-India."   —*Tim Cavanaugh*

At Victoria Station, the R.T.O. gave me a travel warrant, a white feather, and a picture of Hitler marked "This is your enemy." I searched every compartment but he wasn't on the train.

—*Spike Milligan*

FOOD

There are some things that sound too funny to eat … guacamole. That sounds like something you yell when you're on fire!   —*George Carlin*

I have invented rubber food for old people with time to kill.

—*Pat McCormick*

I saw a product in the market—Mr. Salty Pretzels. Isn't that nerve? Everything nowadays is low-salt or salt-free. Here's a guy—the hell with you—Mr. Salty Pretzels … like Mr. Tar-and-Nicotine Cigarettes, Mr. Gristle-and-Hard-Artery-Beefsteak.

—*Bill Maher*

Bachelor cooking is a matter of attitude. If you think of it as setting fire to things and making a mess, it's fun. It's not so much fun if you think of it as dinner. … Nomenclature is an important part of cooking. If you call it "Italian cheese toast," it's not disgusting to have warmed-over pizza for breakfast.

—*P. J. O'Rourke*

Everything has to do with food of one kind or another.

—*Bridget O'Donnell*

Never trust the food in a restaurant on top of the tallest building in town that spends a lot of time folding napkins.

—*Andy Rooney*

Licorice is the liver of candy.   —*Michael O'Donoghue*

I tell my students not to eat anything that had a mother.

—*Colman McCarthy*

Human milk is better than cow's milk. It's cheaper, keeps better over the weekend, and the cat can't get at it.

—*Donald McGill*

Frog legs. I could never order them. I keep wondering, "What did they do with the rest of the frog?" Do they give them little dollies and send them back out on the streets to beg?

—*George Carlin*

I ate more than you for breakfast.   —*Jackie Gleason*

The food in Yugoslavia is fine if you like pork tartare.

—*Ed Begley Jr.*

Despite the fact that meat is made from dead animals … almost all varieties of meat are good enough to be better than vegetables, except veal. Veal is very young beef, and, like a very young girlfriend, it's cute but boring and expensive. … Poultry is like meat, except when you cook it rare. Then it's like bird-flavored Jell-O. Fish—you have to wonder about a food that everybody agrees is great except that sometimes it tastes like what it is. … Most vegetables are something God invented to let women get even with their children. A fruit is a vegetable with looks and money. Plus, if you let fruit rot, it turns into wine, something Brussels sprouts never do.   —*P. J. O'Rourke*

Government

[Government] is not the solution to our problem. Government is our problem.
—Ronald Reagan

My position up to this time has been quite frankly nobody ever told me a damn bit of this.
—Richard Nixon (from the Watergate transcripts)

It is a high ministry, that of government. It is putting Christianity to work, and, by that standard, its success or failure will be measured.
—Frank Murphy

Even *really* disturbed cats do not blame everything on the government.
—Mary Michael Miller

The trouble with being a breadwinner nowadays is that the government is in for such a big slice.
—Mary McCoy

The only thing that saves us from the bureaucracy is its inefficiency.
—Eugene McCarthy

God helps those who help themselves, and the government helps those who don't.
—E. C. McKenzie

Draco wrote his laws in blood; the Senate writes its laws in wind.
—Tom Connally

In the end we are going to be bled to death. And in the end, it is all going to come out anyway. Then you get the worst of both worlds.
—Richard Nixon (from the Watergate transcripts)

We've been creeping closer to socialism, a system that someone once said works only in heaven, where it isn't needed, and in hell, where they've already got it.
—Ronald Reagan

America is due for a retribution. There ought to be a page in the history books of the United States of America of all the unprovoked, criminal, unjust crimes committed and sanctioned by our government since the beginning of our history—and before that, too. There is hardly one thing that our government has done that isn't some treachery against the Indians, against the people of the Northwest, against the small farmers.
—Eugene O'Neill

Giving money and power to government is like giving whiskey and car keys to teenage boys. —*P. J. O'Rourke*

There is only one word for aid that is genuinely without strings, and that word is blackmail. —*Colm Brogan*

The insipid mewling of our politicians is a mockery of leadership. Especially when it comes to the volatile issue of race, creativity has grown so rare, candor so difficult and courage so costly that we are condemned to hear nothing but banalities.
—*David M. Kennedy*

If you don't drink, smoke, or drive a car, you're a tax evader.
—*Tom Foley*

Why should we subsidize intellectual curiosity? —*Ronald Reagan*

If the national security is involved, anything goes. There are no rules. There are people so lacking in rules about what is proper and what is improper that they don't know there's anything wrong in breaking into the headquarters of the opposition party. —*Helen Gahagan Douglas*

Domestic policy can only defeat us; foreign policy can kill us.
—*John F. Kennedy*

I commend the idea of a $250 dinner. This is like the story of the award of prizes by the Moscow Cultural Center, the first prize being one week in Kiev and the second prize being two weeks. For $100, you get speeches; for $250, you don't get any speeches. You can't get bargains like that anymore!
—*John F. Kennedy*

In government, it is much easier to get forgiveness than to get permission. —*Richard J. Riordan (Los Angeles mayor)*

Anyone who thinks Japan is going to export democracy to China must be smoking pot. —*Richard Nixon*

Rape/Violence

You can't joke about rape? I think it's hilarious! Picture Porky Pig raping Elmer Fudd. —*George Carlin*

Unless it's right next door, people don't notice killing and bloodshed. We take it in like the sun shines and rain falls. —*Eileen O'Casey*

Fighting is like champagne. It goes to the heads of cowards as quickly as of heroes. Any fool can be brave on a battlefield when it's be brave or else be killed. —*Margaret Mitchell*

THE ALMIGHTY BUCK

Those who have some means think that the most important thing in the world is love. The poor know that it is money.

—*Gerald Brenan*

I only write when I need the money. I hate to work. If I got enough money, I don't write. What's the sense of making it if you can't spend it? —*Mickey Spillane*

If they're [the San Francisco Giants] losing $798,000, they might as well make it $799,000 and give me another $1,000.

—*Alan Gallagher*

As money gets tighter, I notice that we get more like the French. We're more concerned with style and better turned out than we've ever been, and we've focused on food.

—*Shauna Sorensen*

My father looked at the check then told the scout "Throw in another hundred and you can take the rest of the family."

—*Joe Dugan (on being signed to a $500 contract in the early 1920s)*

LITERATURE

The novel is a game or joke shared between author and reader. —*Annie Dillard*

I always thought that to win a Pulitzer you had to bring down a government, not just quote Tommy Lasorda correctly.

—*Jim Murray*

When we want to understand grief beyond grief, or the eternal confrontation of man and woman, man and God, man and himself, we go to the novel. —*Richard Condon*

THE GEMS

Changing agents is like changing deck chairs on the Titanic.

—Judy Thomas

God created rock 'n' roll so kids could hear him.

—Mac O'Brian Wiest

The mere absence of war is not peace.   *—John F. Kennedy*

We have met the enemy and he is us.   *—Pogo (a.k.a. Walt Kelly)*

Fans, don't fail to miss tomorrow's game.   *—Dizzy Dean*

I'd like to thank my writers, Matthew, Mark, Luke, and John.

—Bishop Fulton Sheen

Art is a wicked thing. It is what we are.   *—Georgia O'Keeffe*

Using words to describe magic is like using a screwdriver to cut
roast beef.   *—Tom Robbins*

Sometimes I wonder whose side God's on.   *—John Wayne*

Never murder a man who is committing suicide.

—Woodrow Wilson

Mr. Gorbachev, tear down this wall.   *—Ronald Reagan*

My definition of a narcissist is a person who is having a great
big love affair with himself, but he can't stand the object of his
affections.   *—Reverend Vaughan Quinn*

If everybody likes you, you are doing something wrong.

—Marilyn Peterson

I have left orders to be awakened at any time in case of national emergency, even if I'm in a cabinet meeting.

—Ronald Reagan

I am not a crook.   *—Richard Nixon*

Money can't buy happiness, but it will get you a better class of
memories.   *—Ronald Reagan*

She didn't know it couldn't be done, so she went ahead and
did it.   *—Bridget O'Donnell*

Never kick a man when he is up.

—*Tip O'Neill*

Man is born broken. He lives by mending. The grace of God is glue.

—*Eugene O'Neill*

The meaning of the story is the story.

—*Flannery O'Connor*

Ask not what your country can do for you; ask what you can do for your country.

—*John F. Kennedy*

Whether you think you can or think you can't—you're right.

—*Henry Ford*

Give peas a chance.

—*Tom Brokaw (in response to Hillary Clinton's dislike of peas)*

Don't get mad; get even.

—*Joseph P. Kennedy*

Never confuse a single mistake with a final mistake.

—*F. Scott Fitzgerald*

Methodists are not noted for their metaphor.

—*Eugene McCarthy*

Paper napkins never return from a laundry, nor love from a trip to the law courts.

—*John Barrymore*

Idealism is fine, but as it approaches reality the cost becomes prohibitive.

William F. Buckley

They say it can't be done. But that don't always work.

—*Casey Stengel*

Whatever you do, kid, always serve it with a little dressing.

—*George M. Cohan (to Spencer Tracy)*

A twenty dollar haircut hardly ever lasts longer than a five-dollar haircut.

—*Wes Smith*

REVELATION

What you don't know can hurt you.

—*John Bradshaw*

I am semi-pleased to tell you that in 6,000 shows, I have walked in front of a studio audience with my fly open only three times.

—*Phil Donahue*

Captain Kangaroo wasn't really a captain.   *—Griffin Dunne*

When we got into office, the one thing that surprised me most was to find that things were just as bad as we'd been saying they were.   *—John F. Kennedy*

McCabe's Law: Nobody has to do anything.   *—Charles McCabe*

I didn't go down there with any plan for the Americas, or anything. I went down to find out from them and [learn] their views. You'd be surprised. They're all individual countries.
—Ronald Reagan

You don't tell the story, the story tells you.   *—Robert McKee*

WOMEN

Women have to be twice as good to get half as far as men.
—Agnes MacPhail

If it wasn't for women, men would still be hanging from trees.
—Marilyn Peterson

You know, I have great respect for all the women I've known—I can't recall any of them having failed me.   *—Jack Nicholson*

Society is kinder to women who fail than to women who succeed. Some men are, too.   *—Sally Quinn*

I want a good girl ... and I want her bad.   *—Donald McGill*

Women who set a low value on themselves make life hard for all women.   *—Nellie McClung*

Women are smarter than men because they listen.
—Phil Donahue

Women are just like cats. To win them, you must first make them purr.   *—Sam (Sully) Gehring*

I know the force women can exert in directing the course of events.   *—Helen Gahagan Douglas*

Blondes have the hottest kisses. Redheads are fair-to-middling torrid, and brunettes are the frigidest of all. It's something to do with hormones, no doubt.   *—Ronald Reagan*

They have a right to work wherever they want—as long as they have dinner ready when you get home.   —*John Wayne*

I got started dancing because I knew that was one way to meet girls.   —*Gene Kelly*

Everyone is always talking about our defense effort in terms of defending women and children, but no one asks the women and children what they want.

—*Pat Schroeder (Colorado congresswoman)*

There are no intelligent women when it comes to men.

—*Marilyn Peterson*

TROUBLES

We are in such a slump that even the ones that are drinkin' aren't hittin.'   —*Casey Stengel*

I knew I was in trouble when they started clocking my fastball with a sundial.   —*Joe Magrane*

The more killings and homicides you have, the more havoc it prevents.   —*Richard M. Daley (Chicago mayor)*

THE IRISH OPTIMIST

The world belongs to the enthusiast who keeps cool.

—*William McFee*

Birds sing after a storm, why shouldn't we?   —*Rose Kennedy*

Hey, life isn't fair. Happiness is a choice.   —*Charlie Quackenbush*

I don't think you can have everything. When they tell me a player I like drinks too much, I say "Good, that's one thing he won't have to learn."

—*Ian McKenzie (scout for the Atlanta Flames hockey team)*

WINNING AND LOSING

Success is not so much achievement as achieving. Refuse to join the cautious crowd that plays not to lose; play to win.

—*David J. Mahoney*

Winning is overemphasized. The only time it is really important is in surgery and war.   —*Al McGuire*

This [defeat] has taught me a lesson, but I'm not sure what it is.   —*John McEnroe*

It is better to be young in your failures than old in your successes.   —*Flannery O'Connor*

I think it's better to come in second than be impeached.
                                  —*George McGovern*

It is important to defeat an ignorant man in argument.
                                  —*William G. McAdoo*

Nothing fails like success; nothing is so defeated as yesterday's triumphant cause.   —*Phyllis McGinley*

Southerners can never resist a losing cause.   —*Margaret Mitchell*

Once you start keeping score, winning's the bottom line. It's the American concept. If not, it's like playing your grandmother, and even then you try to win—unless she has a lot of money and you want to get some of it.   —*Al McGuire*

The important thing is to learn a lesson every time you lose.
                                  —*John McEnroe*

And what all is more normal than failure? What more in common than to rise greatly above failure or disadvantage?
                                  —*James D. Griffin*

Failure is only the opportunity to begin again more intelligently.   —*Henry Ford*

TRICKS

I have learned that one of the most important rules of politics is poise, which means looking like an owl after you've behaved like a jackass.   —*Ronald Reagan*

You can't clobber any reader while he's looking. You divert his attention, then you clobber him, and he never knows what hit him.   —*Flannery O'Connor*

The trick is growing up without growing old. —*Casey Stengel*

Always write "[sic]" after any word that may be misspelled or looks the least bit questionable in any way: If there are no misspellings or curious words, toss in a few "[sic]"s just to break up the flow. By doing this, you will appear to be knowledgeable and "on your toes," while the one quoted will seem suspect and vaguely discredited. —*Michael O'Donoghue*

AGING/GETTING LONG IN THE TOOTH

People are dying who never died before. It's getting lonely at the top of the tree. —*Dorothy Donegan*

I have reached an age when I look as good standing on my head as I do right side up. —*Frank Sullivan*

The hardest years in life are those between 10 and 70. —*Helen Hayes (at 73)*

The lovely thing about being 40 is that you can appreciate 25-year-old men more. —*Colleen McCullough*

How it rejoices a middle-aged woman when her husband criticizes a pretty girl! —*Mignon McLaughlin*

Full maturity ... is achieved by realizing that you have no choices to make. —*Angela McBride*

I wish it were okay in this country to look one's age, whatever it is. Maturity has a lot going for it, even in terms of esthetics. For example, you no longer get bubble gum stuck in your braces. —*Cyra McFadden*

It's a sobering thought that when Mozart was my age, he had been dead for two years. —*Tom Lehrer*

A woman may develop wrinkles and cellulite, lose her waist-line, her bustline, her ability to bear a child, even her sense of humor, but none of that implies a loss of her sexuality, her femininity. —*Barbara Gordon*

A woman past forty should make up her mind to be young, not her face. —*Billie Burke*

I'll never make the mistake of being 70 again.   *—Casey Stengel*

Springtime is a season we tend to forget as we grow older, and yet far back in our memories, like the landscape of a country visited long ago, it's always there.   *—Kay Boyle*

I can tell I'm getting older. I'm starting to use "old people" clichés. The other day I actually told someone I slept like a baby. Like I woke up hungry every two hours with a mess in my pants.   *—Jack Gallagher*

But what's the use of being old if you can't be dumb? *—John O'Hara*

EVOLUTION/PROGRESS

The immense popularity of American movies abroad demonstrates that Europe is the unfinished negative of which America is the proof.   *—Mary McCarthy*

At the end of dinner, it used to be that the men would retire to the billiard room and the women would go into the parlor. Men and women no longer separate after dinner, however. They now separate after twenty years of apparently happy marriage.   *—P. J. O'Rourke*

A sobering thought: A century from now what we know as modern music will be considered old-fashioned. This thought almost makes one reconciled to the possibility that there may not be any twenty-first century.   *—Frank Sullivan*

Quinn; Pat Quinn; C. Patrick Quinn; Col. Cornelius Patrick Quinn; Col. C. P. Quinn; Patrick Quinn; Pat Quinn.
—Patrick Quinn (an aging California prospector recounts the turns in his fortune by the variations in his name)

Only in this century have we seen the hard-earned knowledge of the ancients discarded, almost overnight, in the name of progress.   *—Kermit Lynch*

Things do change—if you let them.   *—Patricia MacLachlan*

If you would be thrilled by watching the galloping advance of a major glacier, you'd be ecstatic watching changes in publishing.   *—John D. MacDonald*

Stories move ahead by conflict. —*Bob McKee*

The kiss originated when the first male reptile licked the first female reptile, implying in a subtle, complimentary way that she was as succulent as the small reptile he had had for dinner the night before. —*F. Scott Fitzgerald*

When it comes to memory, I guess, we are all passing the hat. —*Jennifer Egan*

When you're twenty-one [in baseball], you're a prospect. When you're thirty, you're a suspect. —*Jim McGlothin*

SPIRIT

It's not the size of the dog in the fight, it's the size of the fight in the dog. —*Archie Griffin*

It's shattering when a player loses interest in camp. When you lose your desire to stand around and eat steaks, you lose everything. —*John McKay*

Love isn't just doing good things. Love is the spirit with which we do good things. —*Merrit Malloy*

SPORTS

There's something about football that no other game has. There's sort of a mystique about it. It's a game in which you can feel a clean hatred for your opponent. —*Ronald Reagan*

Old quarterbacks never die; they just fade back and pass away. —*E. C. McKenzie*

Our biggest concern this season will be diaper rash. —*Coach George MacIntyre*

Golf is a sport in which a small white ball is chased by men who are too old to chase anything else. —*E. C. McKenzie*

In any championship fight, the guy only holds the title until the bell rings. —*Gil Clancy*

There are still over 600 million Chinese who don't care if we win or lose. —*John McKay*

When you are not practicing, remember, someone somewhere is practicing, and when you meet him he will win.

—Ed Macauley

Basketball is the smartest game. *—Jack Nicholson*

When you're playing for the national championship, it's not a matter of life or death. It's more important than that.

—Duffy Daugherty

I'll be around as long as the horses think I'm smarter than they are. *—Jockey James Fitzsimmons*

He couldn't fool us. We could hear his footprints.

—Johnny Logan (on evading the bed checks of his manager)

As a football player at Princeton, I always felt like Dolly Parton's shoulder straps—I knew I had a job to do but I felt totally incapable of doing it. *—Jimmy Stewart*

There weren't many [bowling] alleys that would let me come back. I have an overhand delivery. *—John Wayne*

Old-timer: "The trouble with you younger players is the game is just another day at the office to you." *—Cochran (cartoon)*

The Winter Olympics are easier. Nobody asks whether any of the bobsledders are going to arbitration. *—Tim McCarver*

When [John L.] Sullivan struck me, I thought a telephone pole had been shoved against me sideways.

—Paddy Ryan (1882)

My feeling is, I still have some golf left in me. *—Jack Nicholson*

CONFIDENCE

"Cats are invincible," thinks Garfield. *—Jim Davis*

I think it's a good idea.

—John McKay (on what he thought of his team's execution)

My name's John L. Sullivan, and I can lick any **** alive! If any of 'em doubts it, come on! *—John L. Sullivan*

FILM AND TELEVISION

Will somebody tell me what kind of a world we live in, where somebody dressed up like a bat gets all my press?
> —*Jack Nicholson (as The Joker, in "Batman")*

You wanna dance or would you rather suck face?
> —*Henry Fonda (to Katharine Hepburn, in "On Golden Pond," written by an Irish-American)*

They're murderers. I know the law says they're not because I'm still alive, but that's not their fault. —*Spencer Tracy (in "Fury")*

Now all you have to do is hold the chicken, bring me the toast, give me a check for the chicken salad sandwich, and you haven't broken any rules. —*Jack Nicholson (to the obstinate waitress in Bob Rafelson's "Five Easy Pieces")*

That's quite a dress you almost have on.
> —*Gene Kelly (to Nina Foch, in "An American in Paris")*

I was inches from a clean getaway.
> *Jack Nicholson (to Shirley MacLaine, in "Terms of Endearment")*

Can't you understand that, if you take a law like evolution and you make it a crime to teach it in public schools, tomorrow you can make it a crime to read about it? ... And soon, Your Honor, with banners flying and with drums beating, we'll be marching backward—backward. —*Spencer Tracy (in "Inherit the Wind")*

Years from now, when you talk about this—and you will—be kind. —*Deborah Kerr (to John Kerr, in "Tea and Sympathy")*

Where would an Irishman be without a prayer in a fight?
> —*Pat O'Brien (as Father Duffy, in "The Fighting 69th")*

Snakes. ... Why does it always have to be snakes?
> —*Harrison Ford (as Indiana Jones, in "Raiders of the Lost Ark")*

He-e-e-e-re's Johnny!!
> —*Jack Nicholson (to Shelly Duvall, in Stephen King's "The Shining")*

One of these days, Alice—right to the moon!!
> —*Jackie Gleason (as Ralph Kramden, to Audrey Meadows, in "The Honeymooners")*

Nature, Mr. Allnut, is what we are put into this world to rise above. —*Katharine Hepburn (to Humphrey Bogart, in "The African Queen"; directed and written by the legendary Irish-American John Huston)*

A lot of people may not know this, but I'm quite famous.
—*Ted Danson (as Sam Malone, in "Cheers")*

Strange, isn't it, how people manage to ignore those things that they can't understand. —*McGee (in "The Incredible Hulk")*

Better wed than dead. —*Steve McQueen (to Natalie Wood, in "Love with the Proper Stranger")*

I won't think of it now. I can't stand it if I do. I'll think of it tomorrow at Tara. Tomorrow's another day.
—*Vivien Leigh (as Scarlett O'Hara, in "Gone With the Wind")*

What most people don't seem to realize is that there is just as much money to be made out of the wreckage of a civilization as from the upbuilding of one.
—*Clark Gable (as Rhett Butler, in "Gone With the Wind")*

If you passed the pub as fast as you passed the chapel, you'd be better off, you little squint.
—*Maureen O'Hara (in John Ford's "The Quiet Man")*

Out there, due process is a bullet.
—*John Wayne (in "The Green Berets")*

Certain things in our universe are fixed and absolute. The sun always rises in the east. Parking meters are always set to give an edge to the meter maid. And sons never phone.
—*Brian Devlin ("The Devlin Connection")*

Man can only doodle on his napkin for so long.
—*Pierce Brosnan (in "Remington Steele")*

I just can't go to Heaven without Clare. Why, I get lonesome for him even when I go to Ohio.
—*Irene Dunne (of William Powell, in "Life With Father")*

I'd feel a lot braver if I wasn't so scared.
—*Hawkeye Pierce (in "M*A*S*H")*

Life is tough, but it's tougher if you are stupid.

—*John Wayne (in "The Sands of Iwo Jima")*

I wouldn't go on living with you if you were dipped in platinum. —*Irene Dunne (to Cary Grant, in "The Awful Truth")*

The army is always the same. The sun and the moon change, but the army knows no seasons.

—*John Wayne (as Captain Nathan
Brittles, in "She Wore a Yellow Ribbon")*

Win one for the Gipper.

—*Ronald Reagan (signature line from "The Knute Rockne Story")*

There's no such thing as a sure thing. That's why they call it gambling. —*Tony Randall (as Felix Ungar, to Oscar
Madison, in the TV series "The Odd Couple")*

You can't make one thin dime giving people what they need. You've got to give em' what they want.

—*Angel Martin (in "The Rockford Files")*

The great ones are never understood in their own lifetimes.

—*Dabney Coleman (as Slap Maxwell, in "The Slap Maxwell Story")*

Crazy people alphabetize the spice rack.

—*Allie Lowell (in "Kate and Allie")*

There's time to be Daniel Boone, and there's time to be a plumber. —*MacGyver (in "MacGyver")*

You know women—they hear good-bye in your voice and their lower lip starts trembling. The next thing you know you're buying them something fuel-injected.

—*Charles Kinkaid (in "Double Trouble")*

Let's make a pact about drinking. Let's never stop.

—*Hawkeye Pierce (in "M*A*S*H")*

It's a dog-eat-dog world, and I'm wearing Milkbone underwear.

—*Norm Peterson (in "Cheers")*

Spock ... I've found that evil usually triumphs—unless good is very, very careful. —*Dr. Leonard McCoy (in "Star Trek")*

The Tartar woman is for me, and my blood says "Take her!"
—*John Wayne (as Genghis Khan, to Susan Hayward, in "The Conqueror")*

I'm tired of being an object of ridicule. I wanna be a figure of fear, respect, and sex! —*Radar O'Reilly (in "M*A*S*H")*

They're ba-ack! —*Heather O'Rourke (in "Poltergeist II—The Other Side")*

Moonlight is romantic but it's hell to read by.
—*Pierce Brosnan (as Remington Steele)*

Once the trust goes out of a relationship, it's really no fun lying to them anymore. —*Norm Peterson (in "Cheers")*

I don't like being afraid. It scares me.
—*Loretta Swit (as Nurse Margaret "Hot Lips" Houlihan, in "M*A*S*H")*

The first rule of orphanages and Irish families is there's always room for one more. —*Father Francis Mulcahy (in "M*A*S*H")*

I wonder what purpose junk mail has in the grand scheme of things. —*Tyne Daly (as Chris Cagney, in "Cagney & Lacey")*

It's a proven fact that capital punishment is a known detergent for crime.
—*Carroll O'Connor (as Archie Bunker, in "All in the Family")*

Rob, every man makes a fool of himself over a woman sooner or later, and I think the sooner the better.
—*Fred McMurray (as Steve Douglas, in "My Three Sons")*

The only reason that you're still living is that I never kissed you. —*Charles Durning (to Dustin Hoffman, in "Tootsie")*

You're as graceful as the capital letter S.
—*Robert Duvall (to Laura Dern, in "Rambling Rose")*

Well, Tilly, when the hell are we going to get some dinner?
—*Spencer Tracy (last line in "Guess Who's Coming to Dinner?")*

Desperation tends to make one flexible.
—*MacGyver (in "MacGyver")*

Carmine and I have an understanding. I'm allowed to date other men, and he's allowed to date ugly women.
—*Shirley Feeney (in "Laverne and Shirley")*

Tom had always thought that any woman was better than none, while Molly never felt that one man was quite as good as two.
—*Michael MacLiammoir (as the narrator, in "Tom Jones")*

Good night, America—wherever you are.
—*Jack Killian (in "Midnight Caller")*

If it wasn't for art, there wouldn't be any science.
—*Penny Robinson (in "Lost in Space")*

Greed is good! Greed is right! Greed works! Greed will save the U.S.A.
—*Michael Douglas (in "Wall Street")*

Sometimes you have to get to know someone really well to realize you're really strangers.
—*Mary Richards (in "The Mary Tyler Moore Show")*

Allow me to assist you from that ludicrous and liquid posture.
—*Clifton Webb (helping Dorothy McGuire out of a fountain, in "Three Coins in the Fountain"; screenplay by John Patrick)*

I like you too much not to say it: You've got everything, except one thing—*madness.* A man needs a little madness, or else ... he never dares cut the rope and be free.
—*Anthony Quinn (to Alan Bates, in "Zorba the Greek")*

Lizzie, for the first time in my life: *rain!* Give me my hundred bucks.
—*Burt Lancaster (ecstatic, to Katharine Hepburn, in "The Rainmaker")*

Forty-two percent of all liberals are queer. The Wallace people took a poll.
—*Peter Boyle (in "Joe")*

Close your eyes and tap your heels together three times. And think to yourself, "There's no place like home."
—*Billie Burke (to Judy Garland, in "The Wizard of Oz")*

Mother of Mercy, is this the end of Rico?
—*Edward G. Robinson (in "Little Caesar")*

Oh dear, oh dear, I have a queer feeling there's going to be a strange face in Heaven this morning.
—J. M. Kerrigan (being confronted by brothel bouncer, in John Ford's "The Informer"; screenplay by Dudley Nichols and Liam O'Flaherty)

Not much meat on her, but what there is is cherce.
—Spencer Tracy (of Katharine Hepburn, in "Pat and Mike")

Frankly, my dear, I don't give a damn.
—Clark Gable (to Vivien Leigh, in "Gone With the Wind")

Fred C. Dobbs don't say nuthin' he don't mean.
—Humphrey Bogart (in John Huston's "The Treasure of the Sierra Madre")

I call that bold talk for a one-eyed fat man.
—Robert Duvall to John Wayne (in "True Grit")

Only time a woman doesn't care to talk is when she's dead.
—William Demarest (in Preston Sturges' "The Miracle of Morgan's Creek")

A golf course is nothing but a poolroom moved outdoors.
—Barry Fitzgerald (in Leo McCarey's "Going My Way")

You're learning, Cates. Disillusionment is what little heroes are made of. *—Gene Kelly (in "Inherit the Wind")*

As we say in the sewer, "If you're not prepared to go all the way, don't put your boots on in the first place."
—Art Carney (as Ed Norton, in "The Honeymooners")

Back where I come from, there are men who do nothing all day but good deeds. they are called er, er, er, er, good-deed doers, and their hearts are no bigger than yours. But they have one thing you haven't got: a testimonial. Therefore, in consideration of your kindness, I take pleasure at this time in presenting you with a small token of our esteem and affection. And remember, my sentimental friend, that a heart is not judged by how much you love, but by how much you are loved by others. *—Frank Morgan (giving the heart to Jack Haley, in Victor Fleming's "The Wizard of Oz")*

I'd only blow it.

—*Robert Redford (refusing his split of the money, in "The Sting")*

Faith is believing in things when common sense tell you not to.

—*Maureen O'Hara (to Natalie Wood, in "Miracle on 34th Street")*

Get me back. Get me back. I don't care what happens to me. Get me back to my wife and kids. Help me, Clarence, please! Please! Please! I wanna live again! I wanna live again! Please, God, let me live again!

—*Jimmy Stewart (to Henry Travers, in "It's a Wonderful Life")*

As we say in the sewer, "Time and tide wait for no man."

—*Art Carney (as Ed Norton, in "The Honeymooners")*

HEART/TENACITY

Sure, we went 0–14 last year, but we'll be back ... maybe not in this century, though.

—*John McKay (on his losing season with the Tampa Bay Buccaneers)*

Never despair, but if you do, work on in despair.

—*Edmund Burke*

If fate means you to lose, give him a good fight, anyhow.

—*William McFee*

OBSERVATION

Have you noticed? Anybody going slower than you is an idiot, and anyone going faster than you is a moron.   —*George Carlin*

There are no more real Irish cops.

—*David Alan Sheehan (Irish cop)*

Suicide is a powerful subject for comedy. But it is even more powerful if it's shown against a backdrop of ongoing, uncaring life.   —*John Callahan*

There is no present or future, only the past happening over and over again now.

—*Eugene O'Neill (from "A Moon for the Misbegotten")*

All energy forms have sentience.   —*Shauna Sorensen*

We're losing one child out of ten because they insist on keeping drugs illegal and creating a drug business.   —*Jack Nicholson*

If you're at all interested in social science, cabdrivers are able to provide countless examples of the failures of the welfare state.   —*Michael O'Donoghue*

One old lady who wants her head lifted wouldn't be so bad, but you multiply her two hundred and fifty thousand times and what you get is a book club.   —*Flannery O'Connor*

Anyone can see he's [the Prince of Wales, later King Edward VII] a gentleman. He's the kind of man you'd like to introduce to your family.   —*John L. Sullivan*

We also have rockets. Some of them are huge, and their shape is a definite manifestation of man's ego.   —*A. Whitney Brown*

Cats are liquid paintings.   —*M. Malloy*

My pet, the world can forgive practically anything except people who mind their own business.
   —*Margaret Mitchell (from "Gone With the Wind")*

It is almost as important to know what is not serious as to know what is.   —*John Kenneth Galbraith*

Chickens close their eyes from the bottom up.
   —*Mary J. O'Brien*

I was reading "Cosmopolitan," and there was a woman on the cover, and I thought maybe I should change my image. Maybe I should be more like the woman on the cover. How she's posed with the blouse open to the navel, the skirt slit up the side. And underneath, the caption: "How to Avoid Sexual Harassment."   —*Maureen Murphy*

There is only one terminal dignity—love. And the story of a love is not important—what is important is that one is capable of love. It is perhaps the only glimpse we are permitted of eternity.   —*Helen Hayes*

Coaches who start listening to fans wind up sitting next to them.   —*Johnny Kerr*

There aren't enough secrets to go round.   —*Shelagh Delaney*

MORALITY

Vietnam is a military problem. Vietnam is a political problem; and, as the war goes on, has become more clearly a moral problem.   —*Eugene McCarthy*

I shall know there is a heaven on earth when our moral alternatives stop being the lesser of two evils and become the better of two goods.   —*Paul D. McNamara*

Morality is not so much about knowing the right thing as it is about doing the right thing.   —*Charlie Quackenbush*

SEX

You must force sex to do the work of love and love to do the work of sex.   —*Mary McCarthy*

Sex is hardly ever just about sex.   —*Shirley MacLaine*

When turkeys mate, they think of swans.   —*Johnny Carson*

I don't go through many hours of the day that I don't get turned on, although it doesn't mean I'm going to wind up in some sexual expression of it.   —*Jack Nicholson*

I thought I knew all about sex when I was 29. You don't know anything until you're 70.   —*Mickey Spillane*

The thing that takes up the least amount of time and causes the most amount of trouble is sex!   —*John Barrymore*

Going to bed with a woman the night before a game never hurt a ball player. It's staying up all night looking for one that does him in.   —*Casey Stengel*

EXPERIENCE

The problem is that when you get it [experience], you're too damned old to do anything about it.   —*Jimmy Connors*

How life catches up with us and teaches us to love and forgive each other.   —*Judy Collins*

If you're a singer, you lose your voice. A baseball player loses his arm. A writer gets more knowledge and, if he's good, the older he gets, the better he writes.   —*Mickey Spillane*

Mostly, we authors must repeat ourselves—that's the truth. We have two or three great moving experiences in our lives—experiences so great and moving that it doesn't seem at the time that anyone else has been caught up and pounded and dazzled and astonished and beaten and broken and rescued and illuminated and rewarded and humbled in just that way ever before.   —*F. Scott Fitzgerald*

I'd do these disappearing acts. I'd pass through some seedy town with a pinball arcade, fall in with people who worked on the machines, people staying alive shoplifting, whatever. They don't know who you are: "Why are you driving that white Mercedes? Oh, you're driving it for somebody else." You know, make up some name and hang out. Great experiences, almost like "The Prince and the Pauper."   —*Joni Mitchell*

DIET/EXERCISE/HEALTH

I got hit by a Volkswagen—and had to go to the hospital to have it removed.   —*Pat McCormick (on being fat)*

I started smoking to lose weight. After I dropped that lung, I felt pretty good.   —*Michael Meehan*

Exercise? What I think? Haw! haw! Write any damn thing yuh please, young fella, and say that John L. Sullivan said so. That's good enough for me. If they don't believe it, bring it back here and I'll sign it for yuh. But I know it'll be all right and I won't stop to read it neither. That suit yuh? Well, all right. Now have some more champagne and don't say I didn't treat yuh all right, 'cause I did.   —*John L. Sullivan*

I'm so neurotic that I worry I'm going to lose weight when I go on a diet.   —*Grace Malloy Hodgson*

I'm glad I don't have to explain to a man from Mars why each day I set fire to dozens of little pieces of paper, and then put them in my mouth.   —*Mignon McLaughlin*

I can't postpone my life until I lose weight. I have to live right now.
—*Delta Burke*

The second day of a diet is always easier than the first. By the second day, you're off of it.
—*Jackie Gleason*

My car and my body are in about the same shape. ... All that's needed is some preventive maintenance.
—*Andy Rooney*

I realized, in our culture, if you don't have a penis, the only true contribution you can make is to lose 20 pounds.
—*Tyne Daly*

Never continue in a job you don't enjoy. If you're happy in what you're doing, you'll like yourself, you'll have inner peace. And if you have that, along with physical health, you will have had more success than you could possibly have imagined.
—*Johnny Carson*

I've never really known what to do about my muscles. I'd like to look and be more muscular than I am, but there are so many of them, I never know which ones to try to build up.
—*Andy Rooney*

SEMANTICS/LANGUAGE

The meaning of the title is pornographic, but I'm using it metaphorically.
—*Carrie Fisher*

Bums play pool, gentlemen play billiards.
—*Danny McGoorty*

What we say and what we mean. Apples and oranges. Hell, sometimes apples and Buicks.
—*Charlie Quackenbush*

Language for me is action. To speak words that have been unspoken, to imagine that which is unimaginable, is to create the place in which change (action) occurs. I do believe our acts are limited—ultimately—only by what we fail or succeed in conceptualizing.
—*Judith McDaniel*

The word "feminist" is now used most often to divide women from their own interests and, worse, against one another.
—*Suzy McKee Charnas*

When the American people get through with the English language, it will look as if it had been run over by a musical comedy.
—*Finley Peter Dunne*

The Japanese have a word for it. It's judo—the art of conquering by yielding. The Western equivalent of judo is "Yes, dear."
—*J. P. McEvoy*

You better caveat that statement.
—*Alexander Haig*

BOOZE

I'm no alcoholic. I'm a drunkard. The difference is drunkards don't go to meetings.
—*Jackie Gleason*

[Recipe for turkey cocktail]: To one large turkey, add one gallon of vermouth and a demijohn of Angostura bitters. Shake."
—*F. Scott Fitzgerald*

I haven't touched a drop of alcohol since the invention of the funnel.
—*Malachy McCourt*

When it's third and ten, you can take the milk drinkers and I'll take the whiskey drinkers every time.
—*Max McGee*

A drunkard is like a whiskey bottle: all neck and belly and no head.
—*Austin O'Malley*

Just once I'd like to do it sober.
—*Ali MacGraw*

When I realized that what I had turned out to be was a lousy, two-bit hustler and drunk, I wasn't depressed at all. I was glad to have depression.
—*Danny McGoorty*

I drink for the honorable pleasure of getting bagged.
—*Jackie Gleason*

Whiskey and women will kill you. I know they killed my brother. He couldn't get either, so he just laid down and died.
—*Whitey Ford*

It depends on the length of the game.
—*King Kelly (when asked if he drinks during games)*

Drinking is not a spectator sport.
—*Jim Brosnan*

First you take a drink, then the drink takes a drink, then the drink takes you. —*F. Scott Fitzgerald*

My uncle staggered in the other night, loaded. His wife said, "Where have you been?" He said, "I bought something for the house." She said, "What did you buy for the house?" He said, "A round of drinks." —*Jimmy Joyce*

Definitions

A cat is a crossword puzzle with no clues. —*Mac O'Brian Wiest*

An atheist is a man who has no invisible means of support. —*Fulton J. Sheen*

Murder is the execution of someone the murderer thinks is guilty, and execution is the murder of someone society thinks is guilty. —*John Riley*

A writer is someone who always sells. An author is one who writes a book that makes a big splash. —*Mickey Spillane*

Swearing was invented as a compromise between running away and fighting. —*Finley Peter Dunne*

A bimbo is a young woman who's not pretty enough to be a model, not smart enough to be an actress, and not nice enough to be a poisonous snake. —*P. J. O'Rourke*

Optimism is the content of small men in high places. —*F. Scott Fitzgerald*

Chappaquiddick: the name of a place brought up by candidates every time they say they are not going to bring it up. —*Mark Russell*

A cat without a dog is like a lazy Saturday morning without "The Three Stooges." —*Sasha Sullivan*

A farm is a hunk of land on which, if you get up early enough mornings and work late enough nights, you'll make a fortune—if you strike oil on it. —*Fibber McGee*

A collision is a "near miss." … A "near hit" is when two planes almost collide. —*George Carlin*

Personality is an unbroken series of successful gestures.
—*F. Scott Fitzgerald*

To love is to stop comparing. —*Merrit Malloy*

A fanatic is a man who does what he thinks the Lord would do if he knew the facts of the situation. —*Finley Peter Dunne*

A goal is a dream with a deadline. —*Harvey Mackay*

I am a harp, that is my history, Irish and Catholic, from steerage to suburbia in three generations. —*John Gregory Dunne*

Football is not a contact sport. It's a collision sport. Dancing is a good example of a contact sport. —*Duffy Daugherty*

An associate producer is the only guy in Hollywood who will associate with a producer. —*Fred Allen*

A man is not finished when he is defeated. He is finished when he quits. —*Richard Nixon*

MARRIAGE

A successful marriage requires falling in love many times, always with the same person. —*Mignon McLaughlin*

Marrying a man is like buying something you've been admiring for a long time in a shop window. You may love it when you get it home, but it doesn't always go with everything else in the house. —*Jean Kerr*

The first year he talks and she listens. The second year she talks and he listens. The third year they both talk and the neighbors listen. —*Donald McGill*

A man will marry a woman because he needs a mother he can communicate with. —*Martin Mull*

I met my wife in a New York bar. We had a lot in common: We were both from California, and we were both drunk.
—*Tug McGraw*

A wife helps a man more than anyone; she criticizes him more.
—*Henry Ford*

Half my friends said I should get married. The other half said I should get a lawyer. So I'm doing both at once.

—*Edward M. (Ted) Kennedy*

My wife doesn't stop for red lights anymore. She says, "If you've seen one or two, you've seen 'em all." —*Dave Barry*

Marriage was all a woman's idea, and for man's acceptance of the pretty yoke it becomes us to be grateful. —*Phyllis McGinley*

Honesty has ruined more marriages than infidelity.

—*Charles McCabe*

He's never been with a woman as old [37] as I am. He likes me to have opinions and talk back, but sometimes when I do he'll threaten to go down to the high school and look around.

—*Bo Derek [Cathleen Collins] (on 67-year-old-husband John Derek, whose previous marriages ended when Ursula Andress was 30 and Linda Evans was 33)*

I've had an exciting life. I married for love and got a little money along with it. —*Rose Kennedy*

Marriage is Alan's way of saying good-bye.

—*Mia Farrow (of Alan Jay Lerner)*

I am married to Beatrice Salkeld, a painter. We have no children, except me. —*Brendan Behan*

My parents have been married for 32 years. I can't spend 32 days with somebody. —*Charlie Sheen*

It's hot in here. I think I'll take my ring off.

—*Fred Allen (regarding his wedding band, when he saw pretty girls)*

Marriage is a wonderful invention; but then again so is a bicycle repair kit. —*Billy Connolly*

The responsibility for recording a marriage has always been up to the woman. Wasn't for her, marriage would have disappeared long since. No man is going to jeopardize his present or poison his future with a lot of little brats hollerin' around the house, 'less he's forced to. It's up to the woman to knock him down, hog-tie him, and drag him in front of two witnesses immediately, if not sooner. Anytime after that is too late.

—*Preston Sturges (uttered by the deadpan Al Bridge in Sturges's classic, "The Miracle of Morgan's Creek")*

DIVORCE

If there is any realistic deterrent to marriage, it's the fact that you can't afford divorce.   —*Jack Nicholson*

Being divorced is like being hit by a Mack truck. If you live through it, you start looking very carefully to the right and to the left.   —*Jean Kerr*

Wives invariably flourish when deserted. ... It is the deserting male, the reckless idealist rushing about the world seeking a non-existent felicity, who often ends in disaster.

—*William McFee*

Divorce isn't the end of a marriage; it's more terrible—it's the absence of marriage.   —*Mitchell Miller*

PARENTS

First our parents survive us and then we survive them.

—*Charlie Quackenbush*

The thing to remember about fathers is, they're men.

—*Phyllis McGinley*

If we can genuinely honor our mother and father, we are not only at peace with ourselves but we can then give birth to our future.   —*Shirley MacLaine*

Mothers all want their sons to grow up to be president, but they don't want them to become politicians in the process.

—*John F. Kennedy*

I had the total attention of both my parents, and was secure in the knowledge of being loved. ... My memories of falling asleep at night are to the comfortable sound of my parents' voices, voices which conveyed in their tones the message that these two people loved and trusted one another.

—*Jill Kerr Conway*

My mother used to say, "Joe is too dumb to quit anything he starts."
—*Joseph P. McCarthy*

I think my father and the rest of them invented the happy family and put it into movies to drive everyone crazy. —*Jill Robinson*

Adults look at their parents as people with histories and complexities and, often, mysteries that will never be fully unraveled.
—*Patti Davis*

When I first read about my mother and Sinatra in Kitty Kelley's book, I thought, "Well, God, I spent the whole evening with him and he never came on to me." … And then I thought, "Maybe he did come on to me and I just didn't recognize it. Maybe there was something to those singing lessons after all."
—*Patti Davis*

CHILDREN

A child is nature's only bona fide, guaranteed positive surprise.
—*Jack Nicholson*

The kids are it!
—*Murphy (Mary Theresa) McDonell*

Children may tear up a house, but they never break up a home.
—*E. C. McKenzie*

Never raise your hand to your children—it leaves your midsection unprotected.
—*Fred Allen*

There are no illegitimate babies.
—*Merrit Malloy*

The real menace in dealing with a five-year-old is that in no time at all you begin to sound like a five-year-old.
—*Jean Kerr*

If you don't want your children to hear what you're saying, pretend you're talking to them.
—*E. C. McKenzie*

Kids—they're not easy, but there has to be some penalty for sex!
—*Bill Maher*

It's customarily said that Christmas is done "for the kids." Considering how awful Christmas is and how little our society likes children, this must be true.
—*P. J. O'Rourke*

FAMILY

Having a family is like having a bowling alley installed in your brain.   *—Martin Mull*

Our family didn't exactly come from the wrong side of the tracks, but we were certainly always within the sound of the train whistles.   *—Ronald Reagan*

Family trees seem to produce a variety of nuts. *—E. C. McKenzie*

Judging from my experience of having a child, I'm glad Murphy isn't missing it.   *—Candice Bergen*

It was heaven to sit on his lap, and the perfume of my father—a mixture of maleness and the best Havana cigars—was the breath of Araby to me.

—Preston Sturges (on stepfather Solomon Sturges)

There's enough Sullivans to make an army big enough to capture Canada from the British and make it Irish, like it ought to be. There's enough of us to man the navy and send all John Bull's ships where they belong.   *—John L. Sullivan*

Babies don't come with directions on the back or batteries that can be removed. Motherhood is twenty-four hours a day, seven days a week. You can't "leave the office."

—Pat Schroeder (Colorado congresswoman)

WORD PAINTINGS

As a result of starvation pay in the sciences, the class of '91 will include 30,000 new lawyers who will soon be chasing ambulances and sifting through obstetric files eager to rob someone at the point of a pen. It's a depressing number yet barely enough to defend the 150,000 white-collar felons who will graduate along with them. When the Japanese take the lead in the high-tech markets, maybe we can sue them to get it back.

—A. Whitney Brown

If you have a talent, use it in every which way possible. Don't hoard it. Don't dole it out like a miser. Spend it lavishly like a millionaire intent on going broke.   *—Brendan Francis*

Resolved unanimously with one dissenting voice.

—*Irish Board of Guardians (from a report)*

To clear our ears of the shibboleths and cant of the last decade, whose moral bankruptcy now stands grotesquely revealed.

—*David M. Kennedy*

The writer must hew the phantom rock.

—*Carson McCullers*

DISTINCTION

If play interrupts your work, you're healthy. If work interrupts your play, you're broke.

—*James (Big Jim) O'Hara*

Women are stronger at the roots, but on the top part of it, men are surer of it.

—*Jack Nicholson*

Fame is a comic distinction shared with Roy Rogers' horse and Miss Watermelon of 1955.

—*Flannery O'Connor*

If you're worshiping things, it means you're not really leading a full life. It's healthy to admire; all of my musical growth has come out of admiration. But to worship, that's taking it too far. You've got to get yourself together if you do that. —*Joni Mitchell*

"I love you"—that's a hard thing to say when you finally mean it.

—*Merrit Malloy*

Only a fool would mistake the conductor for the composer.

—*Bob McKee (on the distinction between the writer and the director)*

PRIDE

Why, if you was to cut the name of Sullivan out of the Boston Directory, it 'ud look like the Bible would if it didn't say nothing about God.

—*John L. Sullivan*

I completely storyboarded "The Maltese Falcon" because I didn't want to lose face with the crew. I wanted to give the impression that I knew what I was doing.

—*John Huston*

I've made my mistakes, but in all my years of public service, I have earned every cent.

—*Richard Nixon*

AMERICAN CITIES

San Francisco rock, San Francisco writing, it's always real light-weight. Nothing important has ever come out of San Francisco, Rice-A-Roni aside. —*Michael O'Donoghue*

There is no city in the United States in which I get a warmer reception and less votes than Columbus, Ohio.
—*John F. Kennedy*

We must restore to Chicago all the good things it never had.
—*Richard Daley (Chicago mayor)*

Well, it's good to get away from Washington and be back here in the U.S.A. —*Joseph P. McCarthy*

The town was so dull that when the tide went out, it refused to come back. —*Fred Allen*

In Arizona, you can stick to the trees.
—*Larry McMurtry (from "Anything for Billy")*

The suburbs are merely vast dormitories where a man may sleep in comparatively pure air while his office is being washed. —*William McFee*

The crime situation is so bad in some American cities, you could walk five blocks and never leave the scene of the crime.
—*E. C. McKenzie*

Washington is a city of Southern efficiency and Northern charm. —*John F. Kennedy*

Not much goes in or out of there [Moreland, Kentucky], except Charles Kuralt a couple of times a year.
—*Joe Magrane (on his hometown)*

AMERICA/ST. PATRICK

Ireland was born on a storm-swept rock and hates the soft growth of sun-baked lands where there is no frost in men's bones. —*Liam O'Flaherty*

We can do Ireland more good by our Americanism than our Irishism. —*Tip O'Neill*

In our brief national history, we have shot four of our presidents, worried five of them to death, impeached one, and hounded another out of office. And when all else fails, we hold an election and assassinate their character.   —*P. J. O'Rourke*

What we need in this country is a new movement, a "don't do-it-yourself" movement.   —*Andy Rooney*

This American Dream stuff gives me a pain. Telling the world about our American Dream! I don't know what they mean. If it exists, as we tell the whole world, why don't we make it work in one small hamlet in the United States?   —*Eugene O'Neill*

The happy ending is our national belief.   —*Mary McCarthy*

We are a nation of twenty-million bathrooms, with a humanist in every tub.   —*Mary McCarthy*

Maybe this country would not be in such a mess today if the Indians had adopted more stringent immigration laws.
      —*E. C. McKenzie*

This country is so urbanized we think low-fat milk comes from cows on aerobic-exercise programs.   —*P. J. O'Rourke*

A well-informed American knows the lineup of baseball teams and about half the words of the Star Spangled Banner.
      —*E. C. McKenzie*

In America we have an upper crust and a lower crust, but it's what's between—the middle class—that gives the real flavor.
      —*Virginia L. McCleary*

America is the land of opportunity; here, you can get thirteen albums for a dollar ninety-nine. And if you have any ambition at all, you can change your address (and get thirteen more).
      —*A. Whitney Brown*

The beauty of America is that the average man always thinks he's above average.   —*E. C. McKenzie*

St. Patrick drove the snakes out of Ireland, so they all swam to America and became Irish-American judges.   —*Brendan Behan*

This country [America] is Ireland's base of operations. Here, in this Republic—whose flag first flashed on the breeze in defiance of England—whose first national hosts rained an iron hail of destruction upon England's power—we are free to express the sentiments and to declare the hopes of Ireland.

—Patrick Ford

Only Americans have mastered the art of being prosperous and broke at the same time.   *—E. C. McKenzie*

America—a country that has leapt from barbarism to decadence without touching civilization.   *—John O'Hara*

The United States was a pendulum, a nation of compromise held in balance as much by instinct as by constitution, swinging now to one extreme, now to another. The center would always hold.   *—Jan Morris*

It's [St. Patrick's day] a very holy day at home, and since I don't go to church too often and am not too holy, I like it better here.   *—Michael Sullivan*

TAXES

Ambition in America is still rewarded … with high taxes.

—E. C. McKenzie

Death and taxes and childbirth! There's never any convenient time for any of them.   *—Margaret Mitchell*

DOMINION

Don't let other people tell you what you want.   *—Pat Riley*

The woman who has sprung free has emotional mobility. She is able to move toward the things that are satisfying to her and away from those that are not. She is free, also, to succeed.

—Colette Dowling

Don't sacrifice your political convictions for the convenience of the hour.   *—Edward M. (Ted) Kennedy*

I am totally unashamed of my way of living.   *—Jack Nicholson*

I am not now and have never been an actor. Neither have I ever been a crypto-anything; I have always worn my political heart on my sleeve. If I have made enemies, it is because enemies are the children of opinions, and my opinions always have been lusty and unashamed.
                                                                    —*Philip Dunne*

IRISH TEMPER

After you've played for three hours, I think it was unnecessary to disqualify me for a four-letter word. ... I let things rattle me.
                                                                    —*John McEnroe*

There's nothing, I think, that can make a person angrier than anger.
                                                                    —*Sean Penn*

The Irish are the crybabies of the Western world. Even the mildest quip will send them off in resolutions and protests.
                                                                    —*Heywood (Hale) Broun*

If you go in for argument, take care of your temper. Your logic, if you have any, will take care of itself.
                                                                    —*Joseph Farrell*

If a guy takes off his wristwatch before he fights, he means business.
                                                                    —*Al McGuire*

LOVE

I know I am falling in love because I think of you and I turn hollow inside, and the world kind of veers ... like it goes a little bit sideways for an instant.
                                                                    —*John D. MacDonald*

True love doesn't have a happy ending; true love doesn't have an ending.
                                                                    —*E. C. McKenzie*

The trick about love is that we get to see the best part of other people with the best part of ourselves.
                                                                    —*Merrit Malloy*

No one has ever loved anyone the way everyone wants to be loved.
                                                                    —*Mignon McLaughlin*

Love is Tristan and Isolde or Abelard and Heloise or Bruce and Demi or Nick and Nora Charles; friendship is Malcolm and Liz.
                                                                    —*James Collins*

Love's a disease. But curable. —*Rose Macaulay*

I only miss you on days that end with a "Y."
—*Jim Malloy-Even Stevens*

Love is purely a creation of the human imagination. … The important example of how the human imagination continually outruns the creature it inhabits. —*Katherine Anne Porter*

[Love:] A game of secret, cunning stratagems, in which only the fools who are fated to lose reveal their true aims or motives—even to themselves. —*Eugene O'Neill*

Love cannot be domesticated, for it answers to no local power.
—*Shauna Sorensen*

Love is a concept that never gets resolved. —*Bob McKee*

Love is as strict as acting. If you want to love somebody, stand there and do it. If you don't, don't. There are no other choices. —*Tyne Daly*

Love cannot be told what to do, or made to stay home. Love is a wildness in the genes, in the heart, in the mind. It is a direct computer to the senses. —*Shauna Sorensen*

You shouldn't blow the chance when you've got the chance to say "I love you. … I honestly love you." —*Peter Allen*

I found an island in your heart, a country in your eyes.
—*Jim Morrison*

CONFESSIONS

We cheat like hell. —*Father Vaughan Quinn (goalie for an all-priest hockey team, on how the team wins its games)*

Mike Hammer drinks beer and not cognac because I can't spell cognac. —*Mickey Spillane*

I've had many years that I was not so successful as a ball player, as it was a game of skill. —*Casey Stengel*

Truthfully, I've always been a miserable person. …
—*Mickey Rourke*

It wasn't my finest hour. It wasn't even my finest hour and a half.

—Bill Clinton (on his infamously long and dull speech nominating Michael Dukakis in 1988)

I want to tell you something about myself that will help to explain a lot of things about me. You might as well hear it now. First of all, I am a Mick.

—James Malloy (in "BUtterfield 8," by John O'Hara)

PREFERENCES

As far as I'm concerned, the best place in the world to be is on a good cutting horse working cattle.   *—Sandra Day O'Connor*

If it isn't at the 7–Eleven, I don't need it.   *—Marilyn Peterson*

Two things are important in my life—sex and laughs. But, unfortunately, I get them at the same time.   *—Anthony Quinn*

I don't like to be told what to do. It's central in my nature.

—Jack Nicholson

I like young girls. Their stories are shorter.   *—Thomas McGuane*

I hate celebrity hangouts where they charge you an arm and a leg for inferior food.   *—Gerald McRaney*

I don't like going to the dentist. I don't like having any part of a man in my mouth for that long.   *—Martin Mull*

I want to be a prince of the blood and nothing less.

—Preston Sturges (on why he accepted a salary of $10.00 to direct his first picture)

What is broken is broken—and I'd rather remember it as it was than mend it and see the broken places as long as I live.

—Margaret Mitchell

If I had my life to live over again, I would have a different father, a different wife, and a different religion.

—John F. Kennedy

As for me, I would rather be able to love things I cannot have than to have things I am not able to love.   *—Merrit Malloy*

WORK/CAREER

If you get to thirty-five and your job still involves wearing a name tag, you've probably made a serious vocational error.
—*Dennis Miller*

I have never liked working. To me, a job is an invasion of privacy.
—*Danny McGoorty*

Hard work never killed anybody, but why take a chance?
—*Charlie McCarthy*

When I was growing up, my mom wanted me to become a priest, which I think is a tough occupation. Can you imagine giving up your sex life, and then once a week people come in to tell you the highlights of theirs?
—*Tom Dreesan*

There are people on this planet who actually make their livings as sponge fishermen. There must be a real trick to that. You've got to get up pretty darn early to fool a sponge. … Row out at dawn. … Bait up a hook with a messy kitchen spill. … Old guys sit around in the twilight of their lives swapping sponge tales: "He was huge! Biggest sponge you ever seen! Son of a ∗∗∗∗ damn near absorbed me! Huge! Had Comet all over him!"
—*Tom McTeague*

The brain is a wonderful organ; it starts the minute you get up in the morning and does not stop until you get to the office.
—*Robert Frost*

I always thought if you worked hard enough and tried hard enough, things would work out. I was wrong.
—*Katharine Graham*

I'm sick of carrying guns and beating up women.
—*James Cagney*

I don't know anyone who wished on his deathbed that he had spent more time at the office.
—*Peter Lynch*

If I had my career over again, maybe I'd say to myself, "Speed up a little."
—*Jimmy Stewart*

The days you work are the best days.
—*Georgia O'Keeffe*

Much of the world's work is done by men who do not feel quite well. Marx is a case in point.   —*John Kenneth Galbraith*

I don't know what a big break is, but this is an excellent job.
                                    —*Patrick Flannery (on getting the
                                    lead in "The Young Indiana Jones")*

ACTORS

No one writes a script for me. They write a script for Gary Cooper and if they can't get him, they use me.
                                    —*Joel McCrea (after being told about
                                    "Sullivan's Travels" by Preston Sturges)*

It took a long time to come to the realization that I hate acting. And unless someone tempts me with a vast sum of money to secure my daughter's future, I'll never do it again.
                                    —*Sean Penn*

There is no way you can get people to believe you on screen if they know who you really are through television.
                                    —*Jack Nicholson*

I don't know. I've never played a governor.
                                    —*Ronald Reagan (answer to the question of what kind
                                    of governor of California he was going to be, circa 1966)*

He [Paul Newman] looks great and feels great, has lots of money, gives to good causes, is in love with his wife, races cars, is incredibly happy and still has a face. … After having dinner with him, I wanted to shoot myself.   —*Robert Redford*

An actress's life is so transitory—suddenly you're a building.
                                    —*Helen Hayes (in reference to the Helen Hayes Theater)*

Actors are overpaid.   —*Joan Cusack*

For an actress to be a success she must have the face of Venus, the brains of Minerva, the figure of Juno, and the hide of a rhinoceros.   —*Ethel Barrymore*

What writers do is very solitary and what actors do is very collaborative. And it's frustrating and hurtful to an actor when writers won't listen.   —*Julia Duffy (actress)*

THEATER

The theater must give us what the Church no longer gives us—
a meaning.   —*Eugene O'Neill*

[*Auntie Mame*] circulated for five years, through the halls of fifteen publishers, and finally ended up with Vanguard Press, which, as you can see, is rather deep into the alphabet.
                                                               —*Patrick Dennis*

Actors cannot choose the manner in which they are born. Consequently, it is the one gesture in their lives completely devoid of self-consciousness.   —*Helen Hayes*

BLARNEY

I was not lying. I said things that later on seemed to be untrue.
                                                               —*Richard Nixon*

It was all a rumor. I never met the woman.
  —*Sean Penn (attributed to him, regarding his marriage to Madonna)*

There can be no whitewash at the White House.
  —*Richard Nixon (referring to the Watergate scandal, December 1973)*

I want to express my appreciation to the governor for introducing me as the potentially greatest president in the history of this country. I think he is overstating it by a degree or two. George Washington wasn't a bad president and I do want to say a word for Thomas Jefferson. But, otherwise, I accept the compliment.
          —*John F. Kennedy (from a 1960 Michigan campaign speech)*

POLITICS

But I'd rather have one moonbeam than a thousand points of light.   —*Jerry Brown*

I'm tired of people in Washington lecturing us about family values. Our families have values. The government has no values.   —*Bill Clinton*

Nobody is a friend of ours. Let's face it. Don't worry about that sort of thing.   —*Richard Nixon (from the Watergate transcripts)*

Such pipsqueaks as Nixon and McCarthy are trying to get us so frightened of communism that we'll be afraid to turn out the lights at night. —*Helen Gahagan Douglas*

Hart would be the best candidate to run against Bush. And why isn't he here? Because he ****, that's why. Baby, they can say all they want, but that's the facts. —*Jack Nicholson*

It was sinful that Ronald Reagan ever became president. Most of the time he was an actor reading his own lines, who didn't understand his own programs. … But let me give him his due. He would have made a hell of a king. —*Tip O'Neill*

I have only one firm belief about the American political system, and that is this: God is a Republican and Santa Claus is a Democrat. —*P. J. O'Rourke*

Politics is not a bad profession. If you succeed, there are many rewards; if you disgrace yourself, you can always write a book. —*Ronald Reagan*

The animating spirit of the movement behind Proposition 13— and behind the presidencies of Reagan and George Bush—was selfishness. Reagan's and Bush's majorities were largely built on the repudiation of concepts of community, nationhood, and the commonwealth, and repudiation, as well, of the notion that the federal government, which the Constitution had ordained to "promote the general welfare," had any business doing any such thing. —*David M. Kennedy*

How can you possibly vote Republican? I know one farmer who planted corn last year, and then said to his neighbor, "I hope I break even this time—I really need the money." —*John F. Kennedy*

There are instances where it is in the best interests of the nation not to vote the will of the people. —*Tip O'Neill (regarding the congressional pay raise without putting it to the vote)*

Now that the elections are over, nobody has an immediate reason for lying. —*Jay Gaynor*

Politics makes strange bedclothes.   *—Rosalind Russell*

I have come here to ask your help. There's an old Irish saying, "Never send a boy to do a man's job—send a lady!"
—John F. Kennedy (from a speech to the Democratic Women's Club of Queens, New York)

Clinton has been predictably low on concrete ideas, coming down from the hills after the battle to suffocate the wounded with great cushions of blather. ... *—Alexander Cockburn*

As a popular two-term president, Reagan, I think, deserves to be quoted more extensively, even if it makes him look bad. After all, even his enemies called him the "great communicator.   *—Jack Smith*

Don't buy a single vote more than necessary. I'm not going to pay for a landslide. *—John F. Kennedy (joking about his father's instructions during the 1960 political campaign; many people feel that's pretty much what happened)*

You cannot adopt politics as a profession and remain honest.
—Louis McHenry Howe

What the Democratic Party needs is a twelve-step program ... and the first step is acknowledgment.   *—Jerry Brown*

I find in Washington that when you ask what time it is, you get different answers from Democrats and Republicans; 435 answers from the House of Representatives; a 500-page report from some consultants on how to tell time; no answer from your lawyer and a bill for $1,000. *—R. Tim McNamara*

The citizen does not so much vote for a candidate as make a psychological purchase of him.   *—Joe McGinnis*

It is dangerous for a national candidate to say things that people might remember.   *—Eugene McCarthy*

I must admit, it would be nice if I had a few more exciting qualities than I do.   *—George McGovern*

I have consulted Bobby about it and, to my dismay, the idea [of becoming president] appeals to him.   *—John F. Kennedy*

Being a politician is like being a football coach. You have to be smart enough to understand the game, but dumb enough to think it's important.
—*Eugene McCarthy*

That's the most unheard of thing I ever heard of.
—*Joseph McCarthy*

Either the Russians are doing it, and therefore we must do it in order to avoid falling behind, or the Russians are not doing it, and therefore we must do it in order to stay ahead.
—*Pat Schroeder (Colorado congresswoman)*

People would say, "We need a man on the ticket."
—*Patricia Schroeder (Colorado congresswoman, on why President Bush was not likely to select a woman as a running mate)*

There is no proof that Anita Hill perjured herself, and shame on anyone who suggests that she has.
—*Edward M. (Ted) Kennedy*

If I get elected president, it will be an unprecedented partnership.
—*Bill Clinton*

When I was growing up [there were] two pictures on the wall, J.F.K. and the pope.
—*Paul Hill*

There is no halfway house between communism and democracy.
—*Richard Nixon*

I would not like to be a political leader in Russia. They never know when they're being taped.
—*Richard Nixon*

EXCUSES

What was Watergate? A little bugging!
—*Richard Nixon*

I think women force men to be unfaithful. Men are unfaithful by nature occasionally, but not as constantly as I was.
—*Anthony Quinn*

I can't see that it's wrong to give him a little legal experience before he goes out to practice law.
—*John F. Kennedy (in response to the cry of nepotism when he appointed his brother attorney general)*

I was stopped once for going 53 in a 35–mile zone, but I told 'em I had dyslexia.   —*Spanky (Steve) McFarlin*

My memory is full of beauty—Hamlet's soliloquy, the Queen Mab speech, King Magnus's monologue from "The Apple Cart," most of the sonnets. Do you expect me to clutter up all that with this ****?   —*John Barrymore (explaining why he would not bother to learn his lines for movies)*

It was involuntary. They sank my boat
            —*John F. Kennedy (on how he became a military hero)*

CLARITY

Where there is clarity, there is no choice. Where there's choice, there's misery.   —*Jack Nicholson*

If I knew what I was so anxious about, I wouldn't be so anxious.   —*Mignon McLaughlin*

Get the thing straight once and for all. The policeman isn't there to create disorder. The policeman is there to preserve disorder.   —*Richard Daley (Chicago mayor)*

LAWYERS AND THE LAW

We woulda made it out okay if it wasn't for the lawyers.
                                              —*Pete Ferguson*

When the president does it, that means it's not illegal.
                                    —*Attorney for Richard Nixon*

I wonder why prostitution is illegal. Why should it be illegal to sell something that's perfectly legal to give away.   —*George Carlin*

What kind of a crazy world is it when the only person we have to defend us is a lawyer?   —*Merrit Malloy*

Lawyers don't make history, they follow it, all the while trying to keep their eyes on where the power is moving.
                                            —*Shauna Sorensen*

Everybody who has ever said "Talk to my lawyer" put down the phone and thought to himself "Oh, ****."   —*Pete Ferguson*

An unrectified case of injustice has a terrible way of lingering, restlessly, in the social atmosphere like an unfinished question.
—*Mary McCarthy*

A jury is a body of twelve men and women selected to decide which of the contestants had the better lawyer.   —*E. C. McKenzie*

If you can't get your lawyer to call you back, try not paying his bill.   —*Pete Ferguson*

DIPLOMACY

Both.   —*Jerry Brown (when asked if he would run to the left or right of President Carter)*

There are a few ironclad rules of diplomacy, but to one there is no exception. When an official reports that talks were useful, it can safely be concluded that nothing was accomplished.
—*John Kenneth Galbraith*

This is a delightful surprise to the extent that it is a surprise, and it is only a surprise to the extent that it is appreciated.

—*James Baker*

In order to be a diplomat, one must speak a number of languages, including double-talk.   —*Carey McWilliams*

Today the real test of power is not capacity to make war but capacity to prevent it.   —*Anne O'Hare McCormick*

GOD

God don't make no mistakes—that's how He got to be God!
—*Carroll O'Connor (as Archie Bunker, in "All in the Family")*

When men make God, there is no God.   —*Eugene O'Neill*

They reckoned God was easy. They laughed. They don't laugh no more. Some died hereabouts. Some went West an' died. They're all under ground—fur hollerin' after an easy God. God hain't easy.   —*Eugene O'Neill*

Jesus: a spiritual anarchist who prevailed.   —*Shauna Sorensen*

All coaches who lead their teams in prayer should be forced to attend church once a week. The Good Lord has more to do than worry about the outcome of a football game.

—*Duffy Daugherty*

Christ himself would have been lucky to make it past EST seminar training with his immortal soul intact.   —*A. Whitney Brown*

We look for God as though he is not already here.

—*Merrit Malloy*

It is the creative potential itself in human beings that is the image of God.   —*Mary Daly*

Cats are God's way of saying "Gotcha!"   —*Molly Malloy*

RELATIVITY

Ugliness is a point of view. An ulcer is wonderful to a pathologist.   —*Austin O'Malley*

The ones that give, get back in kind.   —*Pam Durban*

A team should be an extension of the coach's personality. My teams are arrogant and obnoxious.   —*Al McGuire*

If Barry Frank can come out of the closet, I can come out of the suitcase.

—*Tip O'Neill (regarding an ad where he appears out of a suitcase)*

It may perhaps be that the whole of our universe, from the atom to the most distant galaxy, constitutes a single parasite within the being of some inconceivably gigantic organism, or perhaps a globule within its bloodstream.   —*Jan Morris*

Make no haste. Drive safely. Avoid overspeeding. Life is more valuable than time.   —*Jan Morris*

RULES

Creativeness often consists of merely turning up what is already there. Did you know that right and left shoes were thought up only a little more than a century ago?

—*Bernice Fitzgibbon*

Do not invest your whole life in one hope. —*Austin O'Malley*

How to write a Johnny Carson monologue in five minutes or less! Here are a few hints on delivery in case you are tempted to try the completed monologue on your friends. When Johnny loses his place, he will usually "mark time" by discussing some point of grammar with Ed ("Which is proper there, Ed, 'who' or 'whom'?") If a joke bombs, doggedly repeat the punch line. And never forget that it's impossible to overuse the word "weird." —*Michael O'Donoghue*

A president should never say never. —*Ronald Reagan*

As the Bible says, "Love thy neighbor." Just make sure her husband isn't home. —*Larry Wilde*

As anyone familiar with modern fiction and motion pictures knows, excessive grief cannot be expressed by means of tears or a mournful face. It is necessary to break things, hit people, and throw yourself on top of the coffin, at least.
—*P. J. O'Rourke*

Rule of thumb in comedy, no dog blood. —*Merrit Malloy*

REALITY

To be more excited by reality than fantasy is good.
—*Warren Beatty*

Reality is not what you see, reality is simply what is.
—*Bridget O'Donnell*

Reality is okay but it's *just* not enough. —*Charlie Quackenbush*

Reality is not for everyone; it is something only Lutherans enjoy. —*Mary McDonnell*

In fact, truth *is* stranger than fiction. It's just not as *thrilling*, that's all. —*Mickey Spillane*

It is by sitting down to write every morning that one becomes a writer. Those who do not do this remain amateurs.
—*Gerald Brenan*

FEELINGS

If you can remember dreams of flying and soaring like a bird, or dancing, or singing more perfectly than you ever thought possible, you know that no second-hand account of such events could ever give you the thrill you felt in the dream.

—*Gayle Delaney*

Enjoy your happiness while you have it, and while you have it do not too closely scrutinize its foundation.   —*Joseph Farrell*

You can remember the second and the third and the fourth time, but there's no time like the first. It's always there.

—*Shelagh Delaney*

You know what you are by the way a man throws you back at you.   —*Carol Matthau*

I never came to the party thinking I could dance.

—*Ali MacGraw*

If the doors of my heart ever close, I am as good as dead.

—*Mary Oliver*

I've never been happy. I don't know who the **** has ever been happy, except maybe Kevin Costner.   —*Mickey Rourke*

Many a night I would be out onstage, and the intimacy of the songs against the raucousness of this huge beast that is an audience felt very weird. I was not David to that Goliath.

—*Joni Mitchell*

I often feel like I'm circling the airport.   —*Grace Malloy Hodgson*

The only way to get positive feelings about yourself is to take positive actions. Man does not live as he thinks; he thinks as he lives.   —*Reverend Vaughan Quinn*

THE RICH

The rich are different from you and me.   —*F. Scott Fitzgerald*

Rich people are just poor people with money.

—*Bridget O'Donnell*

I am on a first-name basis with two authentic Vanderbilts, two genuine Whitneys, and one former Astor, which is darn good for a boy from Pottsville, Pennsylvania. By and large, I think the experience has been good for all of us: the snobbish poor, the democratic rich.
—*John O'Hara*

God shows his contempt for wealth by the kind of person he selects to receive it.
—*Austin O'Malley*

High society is for those who have stopped working and no longer have anything important to do.
—*Woodrow Wilson*

One of the benefits of being rich is to know (for sure) how little money can mean in the actual scheme of things.
—*Merrit Malloy*

It is the leisured, I have noticed, who rebel the most at an interruption of routine.
—*Phyllis McGinley*

If hard work were such a wonderful thing, surely the rich would have kept it all to themselves.
—*Lane Kirkland*

RISK

You must never let your fear of God keep you out of heaven.
—*Merrit Malloy*

Sometimes it's risky not to take a risk.
—*Harvey Mackay*

Those who dare to fail miserably can achieve greatly.
—*Robert F. Kennedy*

PROBING QUESTIONS

If meat is murder, does that mean that eggs are rape?
—*P. J. O'Rourke*

They're deciding elections on someone vomiting. They're picking the Democratic candidate based on whether or not he gets nooky. You put these considerations against annihilation, the rain forest, pollution, aerosol cans, automobiles, and the economy?
—*Jack Nicholson*

If there's no God, then who made Lily Tomlin? —*Merrit Malloy*

If anti-abortionists are so truly concerned for the welfare of a child, why are so many children left unadopted, homeless, hungry, sexually abused, and hurt? Why don't the so-called pro-lifers focus on the living to prove their point?
—*Kathleen M. McQuade*

One of my correspondents has me convinced that the human race would be saved if the world became one huge nudist colony. I keep thinking how much harder it would be to carry concealed weapons.
—*Cyra McFadden*

What we might consider is how we are good rather than how good we are.
—*Merrit Malloy*

We cannot take anything for granted, beyond the first mathematical formula. Question everything else.
—*Maria Mitchell*

Why is the word "tongue" feminine in Greek, Latin, Italian, Spanish, French, and German?
—*Austin O'Malley*

When you consider that the snow leopard has come to the brink of extinction while the Pekingese has doubled its population this decade, it's obvious that somebody hasn't thought this thing through.
—*A. Whitney Brown*

If blind people wear sunglasses, why don't deaf people wear earmuffs?
—*Steve "Spanky" McFarlin*

I was born here. My children were born here. What the hell do I have to do to be called an American?
—*Joseph P. Kennedy*

Would Eleanor Roosevelt have had to struggle to overcome this torturous shyness if she had grown up secure in the knowledge that she was a beautiful girl? If she hadn't struggled so earnestly, would she have been so sensitive to the struggles of others? Would a beautiful Eleanor Roosevelt have escaped the confines of the mid-Victorian drawing-room society in which she was reared? Would a beautiful Eleanor Roosevelt have wanted to escape? Would a beautiful Eleanor Roosevelt have had the same need to be, to do?
—*Helen Gahagan Douglas*

You think it's a good idea to put a wet, drainy thing like that upside down over your mouth?
—*Gallagher (on noses)*

Where would Christianity be if Jesus got eight to fifteen years, with time off for good behavior?

—*James Donovan (New York senator, on capital punishment)*

If we have to be alone anyway, why don't we do it together?

—*Merrit Malloy*

SUCCESS

When you're successful, the thing that attracts men to you as a date is exactly what drives them away as a mate.   —*Carrie Fisher*

Nothing succeeds like reputation.   —*John Huston*

You always pass failure on the way to success.   —*Mickey Rooney*

Jim Palmer's won 240 games, but it took a picture of him standing in his underwear to get nationally known.

—*Mike Flanagan*

There is no point at which you can say, "Well, I'm successful now. I might as well take a nap."   —*Carrie Fisher*

THE ECONOMY

How did Wall Street and Washington sell us all this risk? Simple: They glorified it.   —*Patricia O'Toole*

A record number of savings-and-loan failures left America with a nationwide shortage of flimsy toaster ovens, cheap pocket calculators, and ugly dinnerware.   —*P. J. O'Rourke*

Reaganomics, that makes sense to me. It means if you don't have enough money, it's just because poor people are hoarding it.   —*Kevin Rooney*

In economics, the majority is always wrong.

—*John Kenneth Galbraith*

Kuwait is a banking system without a country, while America is a country without a banking system.   —*R. E. McMaster Jr.*

Planned Economy: where everything is included in the plans except economy.   —*Carey McWilliams*

The meek shall inherit the world, but they'll never increase market share.   —*William G. McGowan*

The oldest rule of Wall Street: Financial genius is before the fall.   —*John Kenneth Galbraith*

BUSINESS

Whenever you're sitting across from some important person, always picture him sitting there in a suit of long red underwear. That's the way I always operated in business.

—*Joseph P. Kennedy*

It's not the employer who pays wages—he only handles the money. It is the product that pays wages.   —*Henry Ford*

If you're dealing with managers, you've got a problem. An entrepreneur is always trying to take something and run with it. A manager never is.   —*Ed McCabe*

Any [baseball-team] manager who can't get along with a .400 hitter is crazy.   —*Joe McCarthy*

The mechanics of running a business are really not very complicated when you get down to essentials. You have to make some stuff and sell it to somebody for more than it cost you. That's about all there is to it, except for a few million details.

—*John L. McCaffrey*

"Oh, what a goodly outside falsehood hath." I think very likely that this is the motto that you people [the Advertising Men's League] repeat in your minds very often, especially when you are composing advertising.   —*William Jay Gaynor*

A committee is a small group of the unqualified appointed by the unthinking to undertake the utterly unnecessary.

—*Fibber McGee (Jim Jordan)*

If I were a young woman with an M.B.A., I think I'd try to keep things conservative.   —*Nancy Clark Reynolds*

By working faithfully eight hours a day, you may eventually get to be boss and work twelve hours a day.   —*Robert Frost*

A conference is a gathering of important people who singly can do nothing but together can decide that nothing can be done. —*Fred Allen*

Meetings are indispensable when you don't want to do anything. —*John Kenneth Galbraith*

The impudence of these corporate looters in lamenting the decay of "personal responsibility" in the ghettos is past belief.
—*Alexander Cockburn*

The question "Who ought to be the boss?" is like asking "Who ought to be the tenor in the quartet?" Obviously, the man who can sing tenor. *Henry Ford*

MANNERS/PROPRIETY/PROTOCOL

Civility is not a sign of weakness. —*John F. Kennedy*

We're living in an age where you have to call a chick and ask her if she'll wear a dress tonight. And they say, "You're weird."
—*Tim Rose*

Wouldn't it be nice if everybody understood without being told, that you need a certain amount of space?
—*Mary Higgins Clark*

RESPONSIBILITY

You are the architect of your personal experience.
—*Shirley MacLaine*

Do you realize the responsibility I carry? I'm the only person standing between Nixon and the White House.
—*John F. Kennedy*

Cats are very straightforward in the way they weasel out of responsibility. —*H. Thomas (Collins) Yu*

The individual who pollutes the air with his factory and the ghetto kid who breaks store windows both represent the same thing. They don't care about each other—or what they do to each other. —*Daniel Patrick Moynihan*

DRUGS

At least when I was governor, cocaine was expensive.
—*Jerry Brown*

Yes, I tried marijuana in England, but I didn't like it. And I didn't inhale. —*Bill Clinton (while Arkansas governor, explaining that he broke no U.S. state laws.)*

I knew I needed help when drugs became more important in my life than my music. —*David Crosby*

Having a wonderful time. Wish I were here. —*Carrie Fisher*

Of course drugs were fun. And that's what's so stupid about anti-drug campaigns; they don't admit that. —*Anjelica Huston*

With enough coffee, you can do anything. —*Robert McKee*

Pot is like a gang of Mexican bandits in your brain. They wait for thoughts to come down the road, then tie them up and trash them. —*Kevin Rooney*

Marijuana ... makes you sensitive. Courtesy has a great deal to do with being sensitive. Unfortunately, marijuana makes you the kind of sensitive where you insist on everyone listening to the drum solo in Iron Butterfly's "In-a-Gadda-Da-Vida" fifty or sixty times at 78 r.p.m., and that's quite rude. —*P. J. O'Rourke*

The way it must be done is, we must generate the programs in which the people are customers turned away from the drugs, not us turning the drugs away from customers. —*Ronald Reagan*

CRAFT/TECHNIQUE

Improvisations can be either a last resort or an established way of evoking creativity. Sometimes a pattern chosen by default can become a path of preference. —*Mary Catherine Bateson*

You can stroke people with words. —*F. Scott Fitzgerald*

Dialogue consists of the bright things you would have liked to have said, except you didn't think of them in time.
—*Preston Sturges*

All you can get from books is rhythm and technique.

—*F. Scott Fitzgerald*

I'm not presenting anything. I'm presenting people moving.

—*Merce Cunningham*

If technique is of no interest to a writer, I doubt that the writer is an artist.　　　　　　　　　　　　　　　　—*Marianne Moore*

I don't believe in craft. I always tell my students never, never, never take another creative writing course. It's most destructive. What is the use of obeying the rules, following the textbooks, if your voice doesn't sound different from other people's?　　　　　　　　　　　　　　　　　　　　—*Kay Boyle*

All good writing is swimming under water and holding your breath.　　　　　　　　　　　　　　　　—*F. Scott Fitzgerald*

I am governed by the pull of a sentence as the pull of a fabric is governed by gravity. I like the end-stopped line and dislike the reversed order of words, like symmetry.　　—*Marianne Moore*

It's easy to lose the energy you need for a long piece unless the characters are surprising you and showing you something new every week or even every month or every other paragraph.

—*Alice McDermott*

When in doubt, have two guys come through the door with guns.　　　　　　　　—*Raymond Chandler (on writing novels)*

It can be a simple sentence that makes one simple point, and you build for that. You zero in on the one moment that gets that character, you go for it, that's it, man, and if you fail the whole thing is down the drain, but if you make it you hit the moon.　　　　　　　　　　　　　　　　　　　—*Jack Lemmon*

I like to think of what happens to characters in good novels and stories as knots—things keep knotting up. And by the end of the story, readers see an "unknotting" of sorts. Not what they expect, not the easy answers you get on TV, not wash-and-wear philosophies, but a reproduction of believable emotional experiences.　　　　　　　　　　　　　　　　—*Terry McMillan*

TRUTH

Only the truth is funny.
—Rick Reynolds

When all else fails, tell the truth.
—Donald T. Regan

Epigram and truth are rarely commensurate. Truth has to be somewhat chiselled, as it were, before it will fit into an epigram.
—Joseph Farrell

Tell me lies.
—Sterling Hayden

GENIUS

Genius to me has a touch of divine about it, a real scribble of the loss of control.
—Shirley MacLaine

We rely upon the poets, the philosophers, and the playwrights to articulate what most of us can only feel, in joy or sorrow. They illuminate the thoughts for which we only grope; they give us the strength and balm we cannot find in ourselves. Whenever I feel my courage wavering, I rush to them. They give me the wisdom of acceptance, the will and resilience to push on.
—Helen Hayes

Genius is immediate, but talent takes time.
—Janet Flanner

CHARACTER

I always have such admiration for someone who dares to be unlikable, who flies in the face of public opinion and public sympathy just to be his or her own person.
—Candice Bergen

Character is the choices a human being makes under pressure.
—Robert McKee

I don't do character building.
—John McKay

I was right where the bullets were the thickest: underneath the ammunition truck.
—Lou Costello

WRITERS

A writer without a cat risks taking himself too seriously.
—Garrison (Kildare) Reed

My dad's a writer. His favorite expression is: "The pen is mightier than the sword," which I believed for a long time. Until I moved into the city. And I got into a fight with this guy. He cut me up real bad, and I drew a mustache on his face. And then I wrote him a nasty letter.

—*Kevin Brennan*

I assure you I am not as good a writer as some of you may think I am. It is you and what you bring to it … the common work that we do together … all this is part of the making of style.

—*Tillie Olson*

If I don't have something to write on, it comes out of my mouth. It's got to come out one way or another.   —*Wendy Rose*

When I'm asked why Southern writers particularly have a penchant for writing about freaks, I say it's because we are still able to recognize one.

—*Flannery O'Connor*

There is only one trait that marks the writer. He is always watching. It's a kind of trick of mind, and he is born with it.

—*Morley Callaghan*

A writer ought to write for the youth of his own generation, the critics of the next, and the schoolmasters ever afterward.

—*F. Scott Fitzgerald*

I know well enough that very few people who are supposedly interested in writing are interested in writing well.

—*Flannery O'Connor*

Writers aren't exactly people … they're a whole lot of people trying to be one person.   —*F. Scott Fitzgerald*

Writers become idiotic under flattery sooner than any other set of people in the world.   —*Frank Moore Colby*

Hollywood has the finest brains in the world out there. But they're up against all these vested interests, and vested interests are the very devil for the artist.   —*Frank O'Connor*

YOUTH

Youth is that period when a young boy knows everything but how to make a living.   —*Carey McWilliams*

While you are still beautiful and Life still woos, it is such a fine gesture of disdainful pride to jilt it. —*Eugene O'Neill*

FEAR

Let us never negotiate out of fear. But let us never fear to negotiate. —*John F. Kennedy*

The thought of being president frightens me, and I do not think I want the job. —*Ronald Reagan (1973)*

Man's loneliness is but his fear of life. —*Eugene O'Neill*

Worry is a prayer for something you don't want.
—*James Mitchell Miller*

Man is wise to fear: it sharpens the sense of self-preservation.
—*Anne McCaffrey*

DEATH

It is a mean thief, or a successful author, that plunders the dead. —*Austin O'Malley*

The only place people got together was at the wake. Everybody knew everybody else; when somebody died, the others went to pay their respects and also to see and talk to each other. It was all a part of the pattern. They were sorry for the family of the deceased, to be sure, but while they were being sorry they took advantage of the opportunity to have a drink and chat with the others who were being sorry, too. It was a change, an outlet for people who led back-breaking, dreary and monotonous lives. And if, once in a while, someone took a few too many and wanted to set fire to the widow or play steamroller in the kitchen, it was possibly deplorable but it was also slightly understandable. All in all, I've always thought the wake was a grand custom and I still do.
—*Edwin O'Connor (Mayor Skeffington in "The Last Hurrah")*

The dying process begins the minute we are born, but it accelerates during dinner parties. —*Carol Matthau*

WRITING

As a writer, you can only win the war on clichés one way, research.
—*Bob McKee*

As far as the question of whether a writer can change the world … this much we know: that throughout history, so great has been the fear of the power of the writer, that books have been burned in the belief that putting the flame to the printed word also destroyed the conviction that lived in the word.
—*Kay Boyle*

To me a novel is something that's built around the character of time, the nature of time, and the effects that time has on events and characters. When I see a novel that's supposed to take place in twenty-four hours, I just wonder why the man padded out the short story.
—*Frank O'Connor*

If you don't keep and mature your force and above all have time and quiet to perfect your work, you will be writing things not much better than you did five years ago.
—*Tillie Olson*

Writing is turning one's worst moments into money.
—*J. P. Donleavy*

Anything that isn't writing is easy.
—*Jimmy Breslin*

Technique alone is never enough. You have to have passion. Technique alone is just an embroidered pot holder.
—*Raymond Chandler*

Writing doesn't get easier with experience. The more you know, the harder it is to write.
—*Tim O'Brian*

I wonder if what we are publishing now is worth cutting down trees to make paper for the stuff.
—*Richard Brautigan*

Writing is a suspension of life in order to re-create life.
—*John McPhee*

I want much more material; I am tired of my little stories like birds bred in cages.
—*Katherine Mansfield*

Writing a birthday note to Lyndon [Johnson] is like drafting a state document.
—*John F. Kennedy*

When I write first drafts I go on sheer drive, instinct, irresistible necessity, in the dark, until I can see where the poem is leading. —*Heather McHugh*

The number one reason why any professional writer writes is to pay the bills. This isn't the Lawn Tennis Association where you play just for the thrill of it. —*Jimmy Breslin*

It usually takes me about 30 years to write a book—29 to think about it and a year to write it down. —*Charles McCarry*

I write poetry not for publication but merely to kill time. Airplanes are a good place to write poetry and then firmly throw it away. My collected works are mostly on the vomit bags of Pan American and T.W.A. —*Charles McCabe*

SCREENWRITING

The key to a great ending is to give the audience exactly what they want but not the way they expect it. —*Bob McKee*

When a good picture is made, everybody's a prince but the writer. —*Preston Sturges*

In film, logic is retroactive. —*Robert McKee*

FOLLY

There will be a rain dance Friday night, weather permitting. —*George Carlin*

I just sit here and make stuff up and they give me lots of money for it. —*Mitchell Miller*

I got into an argument with my Rice Krispies this morning. I distinctly heard them say "Snap, Crackle and **** him!" —*George Carlin*

The corner over by the fireplace looks kind of bare. I'd like to see something hanging there—you. —*Lou Costello*

I always wanted to write a book that ended with the word mayonnaise. —*Richard Brautigan*

INDEX

122

125

128